MAR - - 2016   W9-CKI-035

DISCARD

Peabody Institute Library
Peabody, MA 01960

OPPOSING VIEWPOINTS® SERIES

Teachers and Ethics

Other Books of Related Interest:

Opposing Viewpoints Series

American Values

Education

Ethics

High School Alternative Programs

School Reform

At Issue Series

Cell Phones in Schools

Should Junk Food Be Sold in Schools?

What Is the Future of Higher Education?

Current Controversies Series

Bullying

College Admissions

Medical Ethics

Teens and Privacy

"Congress shall make no law . . . abridging the freedom of speech, or of the press."

First Amendment to the US Constitution

The basic foundation of our democracy is the First Amendment guarantee of freedom of expression. The Opposing Viewpoints series is dedicated to the concept of this basic freedom and the idea that it is more important to practice it than to enshrine it.

OPPOSING
VIEWPOINTS®
SERIES

Teachers and Ethics

Noah Berlatsky, Book Editor

GREENHAVEN PRESS
A part of Gale, Cengage Learning

GALE
CENGAGE Learning·

Farmington Hills, Mich • San Francisco • New York • Waterville, Maine
Meriden, Conn • Mason, Ohio • Chicago

Judy Galens, *Manager, Frontlist Acquisitions*

© 2016 Greenhaven Press, a part of Gale, Cengage Learning.

Gale and Greenhaven Press are registered trademarks used herein under license.

For more information, contact:
Greenhaven Press
27500 Drake Rd.
Farmington Hills, MI 48331-3535
Or you can visit our Internet site at gale.cengage.com

ALL RIGHTS RESERVED.
No part of this work covered by the copyright herein may be reproduced, transmitted, stored, or used in any form or by any means graphic, electronic, or mechanical, including but not limited to photocopying, recording, scanning, digitizing, taping, Web distribution, information networks, or information storage and retrieval systems, except as permitted under Section 107 or 108 of the 1976 United States Copyright Act, without the prior written permission of the publisher.

For product information and technology assistance, contact us at

Gale Customer Support, 1-800-877-4253
For permission to use material from this text or product, submit all requests online at www.cengage.com/permissions

Further permissions questions can be emailed to permissionrequest@cengage.com

Articles in Greenhaven Press anthologies are often edited for length to meet page requirements. In addition, original titles of these works are changed to clearly present the main thesis and to explicitly indicate the author's opinion. Every effort is made to ensure that Greenhaven Press accurately reflects the original intent of the authors. Every effort has been made to trace the owners of copyrighted material.

Cover Image copyright © Telekhovskyi/Shutterstock.com.

LIBRARY OF CONGRESS CATALOGING-IN-PUBLICATION DATA

Names: Berlatsky, Noah, editor.
Title: Teachers and ethics / Noah Berlatsky, book editor.
Description: Farmington Hills, Mich. : Greenhaven Press, a part of Gale, Cengage Learning, [2016] | Series: Opposing viewpoints | Includes bibliographical references and index.
Identifiers: LCCN 2015028556| ISBN 9780737775327 (hardcover) | ISBN 9780737775334 (pbk.)
Subjects: LCSH: Teachers--Professional ethics. | Teachers' unions--Moral and ethical aspects.
Classification: LCC LB1779 .T42 2016 | DDC 370.71/1--dc23
LC record available at http://lccn.loc.gov/2015028556

Printed in Mexico
1 2 3 4 5 6 7 20 19 18 17 16

Contents

Chapter 2: What Are Ethical Issues Surrounding Teachers' Working Conditions?

Chapter 3: What Are Ethical Issues Surrounding Testing?

Chapter 4: What Are Ethical Issues for Teachers Outside the Classroom?

Why Consider Opposing Viewpoints?

> *"The only way in which a human being can make some approach to knowing the whole of a subject is by hearing what can be said about it by persons of every variety of opinion and studying all modes in which it can be looked at by every character of mind. No wise man ever acquired his wisdom in any mode but this."*
>
> *John Stuart Mill*

In our media-intensive culture it is not difficult to find differing opinions. Thousands of newspapers and magazines and dozens of radio and television talk shows resound with differing points of view. The difficulty lies in deciding which opinion to agree with and which "experts" seem the most credible. The more inundated we become with differing opinions and claims, the more essential it is to hone critical reading and thinking skills to evaluate these ideas. Opposing Viewpoints books address this problem directly by presenting stimulating debates that can be used to enhance and teach these skills. The varied opinions contained in each book examine many different aspects of a single issue. While examining these conveniently edited opposing views, readers can develop critical thinking skills such as the ability to compare and contrast authors' credibility, facts, argumentation styles, use of persuasive techniques, and other stylistic tools. In short, the Opposing Viewpoints Series is an ideal way to attain the higher-level thinking and reading skills so essential in a culture of diverse and contradictory opinions.

In addition to providing a tool for critical thinking, Opposing Viewpoints books challenge readers to question their own strongly held opinions and assumptions. Most people form their opinions on the basis of upbringing, peer pressure, and personal, cultural, or professional bias. By reading carefully balanced opposing views, readers must directly confront new ideas as well as the opinions of those with whom they disagree. This is not to argue simplistically that everyone who reads opposing views will—or should—change his or her opinion. Instead, the series enhances readers' understanding of their own views by encouraging confrontation with opposing ideas. Careful examination of others' views can lead to the readers' understanding of the logical inconsistencies in their own opinions, perspective on why they hold an opinion, and the consideration of the possibility that their opinion requires further evaluation.

Evaluating Other Opinions

To ensure that this type of examination occurs, Opposing Viewpoints books present all types of opinions. Prominent spokespeople on different sides of each issue as well as well-known professionals from many disciplines challenge the reader. An additional goal of the series is to provide a forum for other, less known, or even unpopular viewpoints. The opinion of an ordinary person who has had to make the decision to cut off life support from a terminally ill relative, for example, may be just as valuable and provide just as much insight as a medical ethicist's professional opinion. The editors have two additional purposes in including these less known views. One, the editors encourage readers to respect others' opinions—even when not enhanced by professional credibility. It is only by reading or listening to and objectively evaluating others' ideas that one can determine whether they are worthy of consideration. Two, the inclusion of such viewpoints encourages the important critical thinking skill of objectively evaluating an author's credentials and bias. This evaluation will illuminate an author's reasons for taking a particular stance on an issue and will aid in readers' evaluation of the author's ideas.

It is our hope that these books will give readers a deeper understanding of the issues debated and an appreciation of the complexity of even seemingly simple issues when good and honest people disagree. This awareness is particularly important in a democratic society such as ours in which people enter into public debate to determine the common good. Those with whom one disagrees should not be regarded as enemies but rather as people whose views deserve careful examination and may shed light on one's own.

Thomas Jefferson once said that "difference of opinion leads to inquiry, and inquiry to truth." Jefferson, a broadly educated man, argued that "if a nation expects to be ignorant and free . . . it expects what never was and never will be." As individuals and as a nation, it is imperative that we consider the opinions of others and examine them with skill and discernment. The Opposing Viewpoints series is intended to help readers achieve this goal.

David L. Bender and Bruno Leone,
Founders

Introduction

> "Evolutionary biology provides certain insights into the mechanisms of how human life has formed and changed over time, but it can't provide insight into the meaning behind those changes. Yet the meaning part is often what matters in vitriolic 'debates' about the origins of life."
>
> —Emma Green,
> "You Can't Educate People into Believing in Evolution,"
> Atlantic, November 23, 2014

One of the most contentious issues in K–12 education in the United States has been the teaching of evolution. The scientific consensus among biologists and scientists is that humans evolved from other ape-like mammals and that evolution is a powerful tool that explains the distribution, form, and function of all living things. Many conservative evangelical Christians, however, believe that God created humans and animals individually. Given these divergent views of a central scientific matter, what should teachers teach? Can teachers provide students with scientific knowledge while also respecting religious views?

Those who do not accept evolution argue that life-forms appear suddenly in the fossil record and that this shows that evolution did not occur. They argue that debate surrounds the scientific truth of evolution and that schools should teach the debate rather than present evolution as fact. These arguments, however, tend to overstate the disagreements among scientists. It is true that a few scientists doubt evolution: A Pew Research Center survey in 2009 put their numbers at about 3 percent.

The vast majority of opposition to evolution, though, is from believers who object to the theory on religious grounds.

Some states have tried to take into account the views of students who do not believe in evolution. For example, Alabama's state science standards try to avoid the topic of evolution, and the state requires warning labels on every high school biology textbook that includes evolution so that students know that the books include sensitive material. The label says that evolution is theory, not fact, and that biology textbooks should be "approached with an open mind, studied carefully, and critically considered," according to a 2015 article at *Salon*.

This effort may be seen as empathetic and considerate toward some students. However, the effect may be to short-change students and give them an incorrect understanding of the state of biological science and theory. The National Center for Science Education gave Alabama's standards an F-minus because they fail to address evolution. Substantial evidence also suggests that when students learn creationism in high school, their understanding of biology suffers. "Students who were taught creationism in high school know significantly less about evolution when they enter college than do students who were taught evolution in high school. Similarly, students who claimed that most of their knowledge of evolution came from non-school sources (e.g., the media, church) knew less about evolution than did students who claimed that their primary source of knowledge about evolution was their high school biology class," according to Randy Moore and Sehoya Cotner, biology professors at the University of Minnesota.

In addition to educational issues, the creationism-evolution debate raises issues about religious freedom. Creationism often is based on Christian biblical interpretations and, as such, violates separation of church and state. James F. McGrath writing at Patheos, however, points out that teaching evolution can have religious implications as well, since "we are clearly allowing an arm of government to teach children that the religious beliefs their parents taught them are *wrong*." McGrath argues, "We should not flinch at this implication," since "the state in a democracy has a legitimate interest in having its population be capable of distinguishing truth from falsehood, and enter adulthood with as accurate an understanding of the world as we can offer." McGrath argues that some limits on religious freedom should exist in a school setting, at least insofar as teaching scientific fact is concerned, because keeping facts from children also could be construed as infringing on their freedoms.

A 2000 poll by People for the American Way suggested that most Americans support teaching the theory of evolution in schools. "The overwhelming majority of Americans (83%) want evolution taught in public schools," the poll found. "While many also support the in-school discussion of religious explanations of human origins, they do not want these religious explanations presented as 'science.'" Many respondents, though, wanted to be sure that evolutionary teaching did not deny religion and were willing to have creationism, or creationist arguments, taught as beliefs outside science classes. People for the American Way concluded that the public, then, seems to believe that schools need to teach evolution as science while paying attention to the rights and sensibilities of religious students as well.

Opposing Viewpoints: Teachers and Ethics presents differing viewpoints regarding the ethical role of teachers inside and outside the classroom. The information is presented in chapters titled "What Are Ethical Issues Surrounding Teachers and Unions?," "What Are Ethical Issues Surrounding Teachers' Working Conditions?," "What Are Ethical Issues Surrounding Testing?," and "What Are Ethical Issues for Teachers Outside the Classroom?" The authors of the viewpoints debate issues concerning the ethical teaching of students and the impact it has on educational outcomes and learning.

OPPOSING
VIEWPOINTS®
SERIES

What Are Ethical Issues Surrounding Teachers and Unions?

Chapter Preface

Adjuncts, or part-time teachers, make up 76.4 percent of faculty at all American universities, according to a report by the American Association of University Professors. Most of those adjunct faculty members live below the poverty line. Mary-Faith Cerasoli, an adjunct professor of romance languages at several schools in New York City, is basically homeless, according to a *New York Times* article. "For her, the professorial lifestyle has meant spending some nights sleeping in her car, showering at college athletic centers and applying for food stamps and other government benefits," the article states.

Amy B. Dean, writing for Al Jazeera, argues that adjuncts face exploitive working conditions. She also worries that overworked adjuncts are so exhausted and dispirited that they may be unable to teach adequately, shortchanging students and undermining universities' educational missions. "Fortunately," Dean concludes, "there is a simple solution that can safeguard high educational standards and reverse the ill treatment of adjuncts: unions. Unionizing is a straightforward path to preserving the quality of higher [education] and ending the exploitation of adjuncts." Universities are workplaces just like factories are, Dean points out, and laborers need protections in one just as in the other. "Unionization," she says, "will limit the exploitation of adjuncts without requiring new legislation or onerous regulation by merely mandating universities to respect their employees' rights."

Universities have tried to highlight some of the disadvantages of unions and the advantages of the current adjunct system. For example, in its letter to faculty about a unionization effort, Lesley University in Cambridge, Massachusetts, pointed out that the union "would require adjunct faculty to pay either union dues or an agency fee, whether or not you favor unionization." The University of La Verne in California argued that its pay increases were greater than those negotiated by the Service Employees International Union (SEIU) at other universities. The University of Seattle argued that union negotiations would split up the faculty and undermine collegiality.

In some cases, these arguments seem to have swayed faculty. For instance, adjuncts at Webster University in St. Louis, Missouri, voted against unionization in May 2015, though Faculty Senate member Terri Reilly said that some adjuncts may have been "fearful for their jobs" or worried about university retaliation if unionization passed, she said in a January 2015 issue of the *Journal*, Webster's student newspaper.

However, Colleen Flaherty, writing for *Inside Higher Ed*, reports that adjuncts often benefit from union drives, even when those drives fail. For instance, a union drive at the University of St. Thomas in Minnesota was defeated, in part because new university president Julie Sullivan promised to deliver pay increases. Sullivan did indeed deliver on those promises, with minimum pay going from $4000 to $5000 over a year, a 25 percent pay increase.

The following chapter examines other ethical issues related to unions and teaching, both in colleges and K–12 education.

> *"To complete the transition to a domestic economy based on the pauperization of the American workforce, any example of a section of the working class that has decent benefits and adequate pay must be broken."*

Teachers' Unions Can Be a Force for Social Justice

Jesse Hagopian and John Green

Jesse Hagopian teaches history and is the Black Student Union adviser at Garfield High School in Seattle; he also is the editor of More than a Score: The New Uprising Against High-Stakes Testing. *John Green teaches world history at Castro Valley High School in California and is president of the Castro Valley Teachers Association. In the following viewpoint, taken largely from the authors' contribution to the book* Education and Capitalism: Struggles for Learning and Liberation, *Hagopian and Green argue that teachers' unions resist unjust policies for students and fight against the erosion of living standards and protections for working-class people. The attack on teachers' unions, they say, is*

Jesse Hagopian and John Green, "Teachers Unions and Social Justice," Common Dreams, September 30, 2012. Commondreams.org. Copyright © 2012 Common Dreams. Reproduced by permission.

part of an effort to weaken workers' rights. They argue that unions need to resist these efforts more strongly and fight on behalf of workers.

As you read, consider the following questions:

1. According to the authors, why do elites need to scapegoat teachers' unions?

2. What key differences between the National Education Association and the American Federation of Teachers do the authors highlight?

3. The authors suggest that instead of spending funds on Democratic candidates, unions should spend their money on what?

From 1968 until their last strike in 1987, the Chicago Teachers Union [CTU] led eight strikes that won smaller class sizes, medical benefits, sick leave, and more preparation time. But for nearly 25 years the combativity of the union declined, capped by their failure to lead a concerted campaign against Arne Duncan's [chief executive officer of Chicago Public Schools, 2001–2009, and US secretary of education, 2009–2015] disastrous "Renaissance 2010" plan that slated some 100 schools for closure, predominately in black neighborhoods, and converting many to nonunion charter schools or military academies. When the Chicago Teachers Union wouldn't lead the struggle, teachers in the Caucus of Rank-and-File Educators (CORE) organized teachers and communities in sixteen schools to resist closures. They organized hundreds of parents to picket Chicago Board of Education meetings. As a result, teachers from this slate were elected to leadership positions in the Chicago Teachers Union in the spring of 2010.

With the initiation of the CTU's September 10th, 2012, strike with some 98 percent of teachers voting in favor, the fighting spirit of the CTU was revived by this CORE leadership and its activated rank and file. As [Karen] Lewis [president of CTU] said on Labor Day this year, "This fight is for the very soul of public education, not only in Chicago but everywhere . . . our children are not numbers on a spreadsheet. When you come after our children you come after us and we will protect them."

This excerpt from *Education and Capitalism: Struggles for Learning and Liberation* (edited by Jeff Bale and Sarah Knopp, Haymarket Books, 2012) is an attempt at providing the historical and theoretical tools for teachers and activists to remake their unions into a social force that can win this struggle for public education and a more equitable society.

The Neoliberal Attack and the Lies Behind It

The best evidence that unions are good for the public is the fervor with which they're being attacked by the business and political establishment bent on making the working class pay for the crisis. In January 2011, the *Economist* magazine made a full-throated call for an attack on teachers' unions to resolve the global economic crisis:

> Now that the sovereign-debt crisis is forcing governments to put their houses in order, the growing discrepancy between conditions in the public and private sectors has eroded much of the sympathy public-sector workers might once have enjoyed. . . . Public-sector unions combine support for higher spending with vigorous opposition to more accountability. Almost everywhere they have demonized competition, transparency and flexible pay. Teachers' unions have often acted as the Praetorian Guard in this fight. Unions have also made it almost impossible to sack incompetent workers. . . . Even people on the left are beginning to echo these complaints. Andrew Cuomo, the incoming Democratic governor of New York, is rattling his saber against public-sector unions despite the fact that they make up an important part of his base. Davis Guggenheim, an impeccably liberal film director whose credits include Al Gore's *An In-*

convenient Truth, subjected the teachers' unions to a merciless critique in *Waiting for "Superman"*. . . . But will governments have the courage to tackle the root causes of the problem (such as pensions) rather than dealing with secondary problems (such as wages)? And will they dare to tackle questions of power rather than just pay and perks? If they are to claim victory in the coming fight, they need not just to restore the public finances to health. They also need to breathe the spirit of innovation into Leviathan.

Teachers' Unions as Scapegoats

Thus, in an act of political hocus-pocus, the investment banks and hedge fund managers disappear as the cause of the global economic crisis, and teachers' unions are revealed as Roman mercenaries preserving an empire marked by inept educators. The elites have ample reason to need a scapegoat: The year 2011 has been labeled the year of "municipal default" with some sixteen US cities, including Detroit, Los Angeles, New York City, San Francisco, and Washington, DC, threatened by bankruptcy if they cannot find substantial sources of new revenue or make deep spending cuts. Forty-five states and the District of Columbia project budget shortfalls totaling $125 billion for fiscal year 2012.

With state and city budgets in free fall due to evaporating tax revenue, the bull's-eye on the backs of teachers is not really about whether they develop effective learning objectives in their lessons. As education theorist and social commentator Henry A. Giroux writes, "Money-soaked foundations . . . pour millions into a massive public pedagogy campaign that paints America's system of public education, teacher unions and public school teachers in terms that are polarizing and demonizing. . . . Real problems affecting schools such as rising poverty, homelessness, vanishing public services for the disadvantaged, widespread unemployment, massive inequality in wealth and income, overcrowded classrooms and a bankrupt and iniquitous system of school financing disappear in the educational discourse of the superrich."

The myth recounted by neoliberal education reformers has become so patently absurd that billionaires such as members of the Walton family, Bill Gates, and Eli Broad are positioned as heroic underdogs in the struggle for more equitable schools against the unions and the status quo. Politicians continuously lament the falling test scores of American students in relation to students internationally—particularly in Europe and Asia. Just as frequently, they portray teachers' unions as the primary obstacle to innovation. However, there is a glaring contradiction in this antiunion argument: The European nations that outperform the United States have much stronger teachers' unions and higher rates of unionization. Neoliberal reformers also have no explanation for why southern "right-to-work" states, which have mostly managed to keep unions out of public schools, score lower on standardized tests. As Arizona State University's Education Policy Research Unit reported: "Several studies found math, economics and SAT scores in unionized schools improved more than in nonunionized schools. Increases in state unionization led to increases in state SAT, ACT and NAEP [National Assessment of Educational Progress] scores and improved graduation rates. One analysis attributed lower SAT and ACT scores in the South to weaker unionization there." Moreover, numerous studies have revealed that charter schools, which are largely nonunion, rarely perform any better—and often perform quite worse—than their unionized public school counterparts.

If these attacks on teachers' and other public-sector unions are so intense today, it is because they follow a thirty-year assault on private-sector unions. While 11.9 percent of US workers are in a union, only 6.9 percent of private-sector workers are. This means that public-sector workers, 36.2 percent of whom are unionized, at once comprise the last bastion of organized labor—and the next target. Within public employee unions, the 1.4-million-member American Federation of Teachers (AFT) and the 3.2-million-member National Education Association (NEA) represent the single biggest sector of unionized workers in the United States today. From the perspective of the politicians, bankers, and captains of industry who direct the economy, busting teachers' unions is a key component to slashing salaries, benefits, and pensions in cash-strapped states.

The unprecedented attacks on teachers' unions are about a fundamental transformation of the American economy. Those holding America's purse strings are determined to transfer the burden of the Great Recession onto working people. In this era of austerity, even shamefully low teacher salaries are too high for a US government locked in an international competition to maintain its economic superiority, especially with the rising power of low-wage China. To complete the transition to a domestic economy based on the pauperization of the American workforce, any example of a section of the working class that has decent benefits and adequate pay must be broken—lest others get the idea that these basics of life are attainable by organized workers. The question of whether teachers' unions will organize the scale of struggle necessary to defend public schools and their employees across the country is one that will come to define both the quality of public education and the very nature of employment in the United States. The following section, which assesses the state of the two main teachers' unions in the United States, underscores how far we have to go in rebuilding and reorienting our unions for that fight.

Struggle or Surrender? The Teachers' Unions Today

The irony is that far from being the impervious colossus portrayed in the media, teachers' unions—and the labor movement on the whole—have spent the last several decades in re-

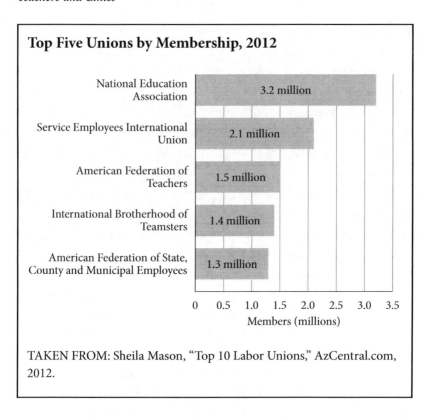

Top Five Unions by Membership, 2012

National Education Association — 3.2 million

Service Employees International Union — 2.1 million

American Federation of Teachers — 1.5 million

International Brotherhood of Teamsters — 1.4 million

American Federation of State, County and Municipal Employees — 1.3 million

Members (millions)

TAKEN FROM: Sheila Mason, "Top 10 Labor Unions," AzCentral.com, 2012.

treat, accommodating many of the demands made by business leaders and government. The "collaborative" strategy of top teachers' union leaders, detailed below, is marked by commitment to partnership with management; unwavering support for the Democratic Party despite that party's subservience to corporate America; and ignoring the possibilities of rank-and-file initiatives.

While both the NEA and AFT have adopted the defensive race-to-the-bottom approach of collaboration with management, it should be noted that the AFT and the NEA have important differences. For example, the keynote speaker for the NEA's 2010 national convention was Diane Ravitch, perhaps the most prominent opponent of corporate school reform. By contrast, the AFT's keynote speaker at its 2010 convention was Bill Gates, one of the most prominent proponents and financiers of neoliberal reforms. At the 2010 NEA convention, delegates passed a resolution rejecting [President Barack] Obama's Race to the Top initiative, while Randi Weingarten, president of the AFT, was equivocal: She didn't condemn Race to the Top, but rather said that it proves that "the federal government knows how to be a lever for change," at the same time giving a nod to some of the "concerns" that the AFT has. Their differences in organizational structure partially account for the different postures of the two unions. As *Education Week* explained, "If the NEA structure gives state affiliates the primary role in developing and overseeing policy among local unions, an inverse situation exists within the AFT, where the central leadership actively works to persuade locals to try out new ideas.... Ms. Weingarten exerts considerable influence over the union's policy landscape partly because many of its vice presidents and resolution vetting committee members belong to the same internal political coalition she supports, the Progressive Caucus."

But while the AFT organizes on a model that concentrates power in the national president and the NEA generally empowers state presidents, the differences between the two unions should not be overstated. Top officials in both unions have made it clear that rather than leading a determined struggle against privatization, their goal is to win a seat at the table to help shape the reforms. The outcomes of this relationship show that the unions have continued to lend their support to management-driven proposals, even when they have proven educationally bankrupt. As New York City teacher and member of the United Federation of Teachers (UFT, the local affiliate of the AFT) Peter Lamphere wrote: "Over the past year, American Federation of Teachers (AFT) president Randi Weingarten has intervened in negotiations between local school districts and AFT locals across the US, pushing contracts that undermine—if not abandon—the traditional core of teacher collective bargaining agreements. In cities like Baltimore,

Washington, DC, New Haven, Pittsburgh, and elsewhere, Wein-garten has advocated deals that undermine tenure, impose un-reliable evaluation systems based on student test scores and divide teachers with merit pay." Weingarten's unwavering pur-suit of the partnership model of unionism even led her to get ahead of the neoliberal education reformers by spurring the UFT in New York to create and operate its own charter schools. Weingarten's reasoning was to prove to other charter operators that they could run their schools with a unionized staff. Unionizing charter school teachers is certainly an impor-tant goal. Yet, by becoming both the operator of the charter and the representation of its workers, the failed strategy of collaboration reached its zenith: Weingarten, now representing both labor and management at charter schools in New York City, is in fact in partnership with herself. Teachers have com-plained that labor/management officials have arbitrarily fired teachers critical of the charter school, and the traditional pub-lic school teachers, who had to give up space to share the building with the new school, have lodged ongoing complaints.

The need for member-driven unions was made evident again when NEA president Dennis Van Roekel undermined his union's resolution in opposition to Race to the Top, say-ing: "NEA supports the plan to limit Race to the Top to school districts. We commend the administration's further refinement of this program, as long as it requires local collaboration, best practices that boost student learning, more flexibility for turn-around models without minimizing the need for results, and as long as it does not reduce the basic funding for children in poverty."

The unions' unwavering loyalty to the Democratic Party has been another factor in their weakened ability to defend public education. The NEA made a combined $56.5 million in federal and state contributions during the 2007–08 election cycle, with the overwhelming majority flowing to Democrats. These contributions poured into the party at the same time that Obama was stumping for the very corporate education reforms that later became his Race to the Top initiative. Imagine the clout that teachers might have had if the union had put the $56.5 million into strike funds for locals challenging contracts that included merit pay, charter schools, erosion of seniority rights, or lifting class size lids. Worse, when Democrats know they will receive millions of dollars from the teachers' unions while they advocate for policies that erode public education, they have little reason to pay attention to teachers' demands. Whether Democrats acknowledge teachers' issues or not, they can rest assured that union contributions will keep flowing.

A New Era

While teachers' unions—and the labor movement in general—have long been in retreat, the struggle that erupted in Wisconsin in February 2011 against Governor Scott Walker's antiunion legislation could signal the beginnings of a new era for US labor. Unions that have long been surrendering to management's offensive were compelled to take action by the prospect that these new laws would destroy their organizations. With state governments across the country proposing similar legislation against the bargaining rights of public-sector workers, Wisconsin workers' struggle to preserve trade unions demonstrated an awakening of class solidarity and action, even though it ultimately suffered a legislative defeat. To be sure, progress on class solidarity and action has been halting. While entire unions entered into mass action to defend collective bargaining rights, many of Wisconsin's public-sector unions have since agreed to concessionary contracts, following the logic that concessions are the high price to pay for salvaging the union at all.

But thousands of teachers have drawn important conclusions from their own direct participation in the rallies, sick-outs, and occupations in Madison and elsewhere, demonstrating that mass collective action holds promise for reanimating the entire labor movement. One teacher in the Madison Public Schools reflected on her experience of deciding to occupy the state capitol in opposition to Governor Walker's union-busting legislation: "Shutting down the state seems really scary to me.... [And yet] when I'm in the capitol, I love just walking around and talking to people from everywhere. The solidarity and camaraderie are amazing. You turn to your left, turn to your right, and you can chat with people who've come to support us from all over the state, and all over the world." As part of Occupy Wall Street (and what is coming to be known as the "Occupy movement"), which began in September 2011, teachers all over the country have participated in protests and teach-ins at banks to highlight how banks got bailed out during the Great Recession rather than schools, even though banks precipitated the crisis through predatory lending practices.

> "The real problem with our education system in this country is the teachers' unions."

Teachers' Unions Hurt America

John Hawkins

John Hawkins runs Right Wing News and Linkiest; he writes two weekly columns for Townhall. *In the following viewpoint, he argues that labor conditions are no longer exploitive and that unions, therefore, are no longer necessary. Instead of helping workers, he argues, unions now encourage wasteful spending and undermine competitiveness. Teachers' unions, he says, protect poor-performing teachers, and public unions in general encourage spending on pensions that bankrupt state and local governments. He argues that because of such problems, public employee unions such as teachers' unions should not be allowed.*

As you read, consider the following questions:

1. What abuses does Hawkins say unions helped to end?

John Hawkins, "5 Reasons Unions Are Bad for America," *Townhall*, March 8, 2011. Townhall.com. Copyright © 2011 John Hawkins. Reproduced by permission.

2. What is Hawkins's argument for outlawing public sector unions?

3. Why are unions undemocratic, according to Hawkins?

At one time in this country, there were few workplace safety laws, few restraints on employers, and incredibly exploitive working conditions that ranged from slavery, to sharecropping, to putting children in dangerous working conditions. Unions, to their everlasting credit, helped play an important role in leveling the playing field for workers.

No More Need for Unions

However, as the laws changed, there was less and less need for unions. Because of that, union membership shrank. In response, the unions became more explicitly involved in politics. Over time, they managed to co-opt the Democratic Party, pull their strings, and rewrite our labor laws in their favor.

As Lord Acton [Sir John Dalberg-Acton, an English historian, politician, and writer] noted, "*Power tends to corrupt*," and that has certainly been true for the unions. Unions have become selfish, extremely greedy, and even thuggish in their never-ending quest to take in as much as they can for themselves, at the expense of everyone else who crosses their path.

That's why today, unions have changed from organizations that "look out for the little guy" into the largest, most rapacious special interest group in the entire country. Where unions go, disaster usually follows. Just to name a few examples:

1) Unions are severely damaging whole industries: How is it that GM [General Motors Company] and Chrysler got into such lousy shape that they had to be bailed out? There's a simple answer: The unions. The massive pensions the car companies paid out raised their costs so much that they were limited to building more expensive cars to try to get their money back. They couldn't even do a great job of building those cars because utterly ridiculous union rules prevented them from using their labor efficiently. America created the automobile industry, but American unions are strangling it to death. Unions also wrecked the steel and textile industries and have helped drive manufacturing jobs overseas. They're crippling the airline industry and, of course, we can't forget that . . .

2) Unions are ruining public education: Every few years, it's the same old story. The teachers' unions claim that public education in this country is dramatically underfunded and if they just had more money, they could turn it around. Taxpayer money then pours into our schools like a waterfall and . . . there's no improvement. A few years later, when people have forgotten the last spending spree on education, the process is repeated.

However, the real problem with our education system in this country is the teachers' unions. They do everything possible to prevent schools not only from firing lousy teachers but also from rewarding talented teachers. Merit pay? The unions hate it. Private schools? Even though everyone knows they deliver a better education than our public schools, unions fight to keep as many kids as possible locked in failing public schools. In Wisconsin, we've had whole schools shutting down so that lazy teachers can waste their time protesting on the taxpayers' dime. Want to improve education in this country? Then you've got to take on the teachers' unions.

Undemocratic and Un-American

3) Unions are costing you billions of tax dollars: Let's put it plain and simple: Government workers shouldn't be allowed to unionize. Period.

Why?

Because you elect representatives to look out for your interests.

Early American Unions

The early American labor organizations were based on handicraft technologies such as shoemaking, stonecutting, carpentry, hat finishing, and printing. Their membership was composed of skilled laborers organized along the lines of individual crafts. Today, such organizations are known as craft unions. It is not surprising that organized labor began with highly skilled, strategically situated workers, because they were the first to enjoy what is referred to today as bargaining power.

Public policy toward early labor organizations was, to put it kindly, suppressive. Unions had no legal basis for existence and were considered "criminal conspiracies in restraint of trade" under common law. This criminal conspiracy doctrine emerged from a court case involving cordwainers, in which a judge ruled it illegal for Philadelphia, Pennsylvania, shoemakers to act collectively in efforts to raise their wages. Several of the early craft unions were prosecuted for criminal conspiracy, but the doctrine was brought to an end by the Massachusetts court decision of *Commonwealth v. Hunt* (1842), which held that such organized labor activities were lawful.

Richard C. Kearney and Patrice M. Mareschal,
Labor Relations in the Public Sector.
5th ed. Boca Raton, FL: Taylor & Francis, 2014.

It's obviously in your interest to pay as little as possible to government workers, to keep their benefits as low as possible, and to hire as few of them as possible to do the job. However, because the Democratic Party and the unions are in bed with each other, this entire process has been turned on its ear. Instead of looking out for your interests, Democrats try to hire as many government workers as possible, pay them as much as possible, and give them benefits that are as generous as possible, all so that union workers will do more to get them reelected.

In other words, the Democratic Party and the unions are engaged in an open conspiracy to defraud the American taxpayer. There's no way that the American people should allow that to continue.

4) Unions are fundamentally anti-democratic: How in the world did we get to the point where people can be forced to join a union just to get a job at certain places? Then, after they're dragooned into the union, they have no choice other than to pay dues that are used for political activities, which the unwilling dues-paying member may oppose.

Add to that the fact that the Democrats and the government unions collaborate to subvert democracy at the expense of the taxpayer and it's not a pretty picture. Worse yet, unions have gotten so voracious that they even want to do away with the secret ballot, via card check, so they can openly bully people into joining unions. The way unions behave in this country is undemocratic, un-American, and it should trouble anyone who cares about freedom and individual rights.

Bankrupting Local Governments

5) Government unions are bankrupting cities and states: Government unions have bled billions from taxpayers nationally, but the damage they're doing on the local level is even worse. We have cities and states all across the country that are so behind on their bills that there have been genuine discussions about bankruptcy. There are a lot of irresponsible financial policies that have helped contribute to that sorry state of affairs, but unquestionably, the biggest backbreakers can be directly traced back to the unions.

As the *Washington Times* has noted, union pensions are crushing budgets all across the country.

Yet it comes as little surprise that the same profligacy that pervades the corridors of federal power infects this country's 87,000 state, county and municipal governments and school districts. By 2013, the amount of retirement money promised to employees of these public entities will exceed cash on hand by more than a trillion dollars.

So, what happens when these pensions can't be paid? They will come to the taxpayers with their hands out. When they stroll forward with their beggar's bowl in hand, the American people should keep their wallets in their pockets. That may not seem fair, but the public-sector union members have gotten a great deal at everyone else's expense for a long time and if somebody has to take a haircut, and they do, it should be the union members instead of the taxpayers they've been bilking for so long.

| "Yes, Wisconsin has great schools, with great outcomes. Yes, states without teachers' unions lag behind."

Teachers' Unions Help Students

Susan Troller

Susan Troller is a writer for the Capital Times *newspaper in Madison, Wisconsin. In the following viewpoint, she says that data on the relative success of students in states with teachers' unions and those without teachers' unions are difficult to find. However, she says that the best existing data show that Wisconsin, a state with teachers' unions, does significantly better on test scores than states without such unions. She concludes that eliminating unions in Wisconsin will harm learning outcomes.*

As you read, consider the following questions:

1. Who is Glenn Grothman, and how does he believe teachers' unions affect student outcomes?

2. Why does Angus Johnston say the Democrats' pro-union argument for teachers is flawed?

Susan Troller, "Chalkboard: Do Students Benefit from Teachers Unions?," Madison.com, February 22, 2011. Copyright © 2011 Madison.com. Reproduced by permission.

3. How did states without teachers' unions do on the National Assessment of Educational Progress tests, according to Troller?

In the heated debate surrounding [Wisconsin] Gov. Scott Walker's proposal to eliminate nearly all parts of collective bargaining for teachers and other public employees, there hasn't been much discussion about what impact these changes could have on students.

How Are Children Affected?

It seems an odd oversight, given that delivering high-quality education to students is the whole point of a school system. It's also one of the fundamental underpinnings of a successful democracy.

Here's a question I've not heard addressed during the talk about getting rid of collective bargaining in Wisconsin: What impact does a teachers' union have on student performance?

One of the most persistent critics of public education in Wisconsin is Sen. Glenn Grothman (R-West Bend) who spoke on the air to radio host John "Sly" Sylvester last week [in February 2011]. Here's what he had to say: "You have to remember, the quality of education in this state has dropped since Lee Dreyfus and Tommy Thompson were governor. I was looking at the most recent NAEP [National Assessment of Educational Progress] test scores; nationally, when I was a child, they used to say Wisconsin had good schools. After the strong unionization over the last 30–40 years, our 4th grade reading test scores are below the national average."

Obviously, Grothman weighs in on the "unions are bad for kids" side of the debate, which will not come as a surprise to anyone who has spoken to him for more than three minutes.

In sharp contrast, there were many tweets from the Wisconsin Democratic Party over the weekend claiming that Wisconsin's SAT/ACT scores were second in the U.S. and that

The NAEP and Student Achievement

I am willing to bet that most elected officials and journalists today would have a hard time scoring well on the NAEP [National Assessment of Educational Progress] tests administered across the nation to our students. Every time I hear elected officials or pundits complain about test scores, I want to ask them to take the same tests and publish their scores. I don't expect that any of them would accept the challenge.

Critics may find this hard to believe, but students in American public schools today are studying and mastering far more difficult topics in science and mathematics than their peers forty or fifty years ago. People who doubt this should review the textbooks in common use then and now or look at the tests then and now. If they are still in doubt, I invite them to go to the NAEP website and review the questions in math and science for eighth-grade students. The questions range from easy to very difficult. Surely an adult should be able to answer them all, right? You are likely to learn, if you try this experiment, that the difficulty and complexity of what is taught today far exceed anything the average student encountered in school decades ago.

Diane Ravitch,
Reign of Error: The Hoax of the Privatization Movement
and the Danger to America's Public Schools.
New York: Alfred A. Knopf, 2013.

five states with no teacher union bargaining rights—South Carolina, North Carolina, Virginia, Texas and Georgia—had bottom-of-the-barrel scores.

So where's the truth of the matter? Do children who attend public schools with unionized teachers suffer or benefit from the experience? Is there anything beyond anecdotal evidence? Can you find the answer in standardized test scores? Graduation rates? Or in scenes from popular film documentaries like *Waiting for "Superman"* with its indictment of teachers' unions?

What I know for sure is that liars can figure, figures can lie, and my own number-crunching powers are woefully limited. So I tried to find a source for data that seemed knowledgeable and fair-minded.

Wisconsin Test Scores Are High

In a blog post on Sunday, Angus Johnston, an American history professor at the City University of New York, describes the Dems' pro-union tweets as flawed by outdated statistics and improper statistical analysis. Then he asks what "good" data could tell us about the question of whether teachers' unions provide any benefit to students.

After taking a harder look at the kind of data the Dems were touting as well as other student performance data, Johnston confirmed in a blog post Monday that Wisconsin does, indeed, rank near the top of the country on SAT/ACT scores. By contrast, Virginia is near the middle of the national rankings pack, and the rest of the no-union states are near the bottom. The same relative rankings are true on another standard of student success: high school graduation.

Furthermore, Johnston had different takes on the data Grothman believes is evidence of the foundering Wisconsin public schools.

In fact, after looking at the very same data Grothman was citing, plus the SAT/ACT scores and student graduation rates, here's what Johnston concluded:

> "Yes, Wisconsin has great schools, with great outcomes. Yes, states without teachers' unions lag behind. Yes, that lag persists even when you control for demographic variables. . . .

And yes, Virginia, (and Texas, Georgia, and North and South Carolina) unions do work." . . .

Now, what Grothman says is that Wisconsin used to have top-notch readers in the fourth grade, and now they're only average (actually, by scores, a little above average). But there were also many more non-native English speakers in Wisconsin in 2009 than 1969, for example, and average income in Wisconsin was in better shape then, too. Despite those demographic changes, however, there are some other test scores that are actually very encouraging, which Grothman does not note (but that Johnston includes in his examination).

For example, what's known as the "nation's report card," the National Assessment of Educational Progress (NAEP) showed that Wisconsin students in 2009 were above the national average in three of four measures: fourth-grade math and eighth-grade math and reading. (Fourth-grade reading scores, as noted above, were slightly above average.) According to Johnston's analysis, "Of the ten states in the US without teachers' unions, only one—Virginia—had NAEP results above the national average, and four—Arizona, Alabama, Louisiana, and Mississippi—were in the bottom quintile."

There's plenty of other intriguing information in Johnston's Monday blog, including his reference to a statistical analysis of state SAT/ACT scores written by three professors about a decade ago and published in the *Harvard Educational Review*. Controlling for factors like race, median income, and parental education, they found that going to school in a union state correlates with higher test scores, averaging, for example, about a 50-point increase on the SAT.

So, when it comes to collective bargaining and teachers, do we want Wisconsin's children in a Race to the Top, or a Race to the Bottom, right alongside those southern states with pretty dismal academic performance? Maybe we need to ask our legislators.

> *"Teachers' unions are the biggest obstacle to educational reforms that would give millions of children a better education and a fighting chance at a better life."*

Teachers' Unions Hurt Students

Akash Chougule

Akash Chougule is a policy analyst at Americans for Prosperity. In the following viewpoint, he argues that teachers' unions hurt students by forcing schools to retain bad teachers. He also argues that teachers' unions oppose the creation of charter schools; this restricts school choice and harms black, Latino, and poor children who are disproportionately served by poorly performing schools. Chougule says that public opinion is turning against teachers' unions, and this will ultimately improve education for students.

As you read, consider the following questions:

1. Why did nine students sue the state of California in Los Angeles Superior Court, according to Chougule?

Akash Chougule, "Fighting Back Against Teachers Unions: Saving Education in America," TheBlaze.com, June 19, 2014. Copyright © 2014 TheBlaze Inc. Reproduced by permission.

2. Based on the statistics Chougule provides, how much more likely are black and Latino students to be taught by the worst teachers?

3. What is the reason Chougule gives for the loss of members by the National Education Association?

Increasingly, people across the country are beginning to realize that teachers' unions are the biggest obstacle to educational reforms that would give millions of children a better education and a fighting chance at a better life.

Protecting Bad Teachers

To be clear, there is a mile-wide difference between teachers and teachers' unions. Great teachers are performing one of our nation's foremost duties and deserve to be rewarded accordingly. Unfortunately, unions have long supported policies that protect bad teachers at the expense of dedicated educators and students—but that all may have changed last week [in June 2014] in California.

In a case brought forth by nine frustrated students, Los Angeles Superior Court judge Rolf M. Treu ruled several of the state's union-backed teacher tenure and dismissal processes unconstitutional and accused them of causing unequal opportunities. The rules made it virtually impossible to fire a bad teacher after two years and could have resulted in new, great teachers being laid off in the event that cuts were necessary. Treu called the laws "unfathomable and therefore constitutionally unsupportable."

Likewise, teachers' unions have long opposed expanding school choice, which would give low-income and minority students greater opportunity to leave failing schools and utilize other educational options like charters and private schools. Like eliminating teacher tenure, school choice would add accountability and opportunity that goes against the special interests of unions.

School Choice Is Needed

Sadly, tenure rules and opposition to school choice hurt students who need help the most and teachers who deserve it most. Latino students are 68 percent more likely than white students to be taught by the worst teachers, and black students are 43 percent more likely. And it was predetermined union pay schedules that dictated that Michigan's "teacher of the year" was one of the lowest paid in his district.

As a result of opposing policies with such commonsense widespread appeal and popularity, public opinion of unions is falling fast. Forty-three percent believe they have a negative effect on public schools, up from 31 percent in 2009, according to *Politico*. One expert explained, "People increasingly view teachers' unions as a problem, or *the* problem."

Even supposed allies are hitting teachers' unions. Rep. George Miller (D-Cali.) called the policies "indefensible." President Barack Obama's secretary of education and the *New York Times* editorial board both applauded the ruling.

As one Democratic operative opined, "It will be very difficult for Democrats to make the case that they are on the side of civil rights and social justice if they are defending unconstitutional laws that objectively harm poor kids and children of color."

Perhaps worse yet, even their own members are questioning teachers' unions. The National Education Association has lost 230,000 members (7 percent of its total) in recent years. Increasing numbers of educators are realizing they do not need to be represented by a body that hurts eager students and holds back great teachers while stuffing the pockets of union bosses and campaign coffers with their hard-earned dollars.

It is a vicious cycle. Teachers feel as though the unions are no longer serving to benefit them nor the kids, so they are leaving. But in order to keep their clout, teachers' unions are spreading their tentacles into the realms of various nonteaching professions—further alienating teachers. It appears the only ones who remain loyal to unions are union bosses and the politicians who depend on them.

The California ruling was the latest blow to teachers' unions who are seeing their reputation crumble with each passing school year. From their treatment of public school teachers to their opposition of school choice, unions are being seen as a burdensome force holding back the improvement of American education—and teachers, families, and students alike have begun to digest this important lesson.

Winter Hall, a frustrated parent explained, "it always comes off like the unions serve themselves—like it's not about the education of the children." Beatriz Vergara, one of the students who brought the lawsuit, recalled one year with a particularly awful teacher a "lost opportunity."

There is no war on teachers. There is a war to save our schools, save our children, and save our future—so that not a single child in America has to cope with "lost opportunity" in our education system.

| "Herein lies the cause of current conflicts with teachers' unions. They, like schools, are products of the industrial era."

Teachers' Unions Are Not Evil, Just Out of Date

Arthur Levine

Arthur Levine is the president of the Woodrow Wilson National Fellowship Foundation and a former president of Teachers College, Columbia University. In the following viewpoint, he argues that teachers' unions grew out of an industrial era in which education was viewed as a standardized process. Unions need to be rethought to address the needs of an information economy, in which student outcomes are more important than a single process, Levine says. He concludes that if teachers' unions don't change, they will become irrelevant and will be left behind by progress.

As you read, consider the following questions:

1. According to Levine, over which issues have government and teachers' unions battled?

Arthur Levine, "The Plight of Teachers' Unions," *Education Week*, May 7, 2013. Edweek.org. Copyright © 2013 Education Week. Reproduced by permission.

2. What epitomizes the work approach of industrial societies, according to Levine?

3. What other social institutions does Levine say were created for an industrial economy?

In late March [2013], Karen Lewis, the president of the Chicago Teachers Union, attacked Mayor Rahm Emanuel for undermining the city's schools with a plan to close more than 50 underutilized schools. Earlier this year, Mayor Michael R. Bloomberg of New York blamed the local teachers' union for the loss of millions in federal funds, resulting from its unwillingness to accept outcome-based teacher evaluation.

Under Siege

Teachers' unions are under siege nationwide. Criticism by political leaders and education reformers has snowballed. In recent years, government and unions have battled over tenure, teacher assessment, testing, the length of the school day, class size, school closures, and pay for performance. The hottest issues have dealt with reliance on teacher seniority as the basis for job assignments, retrenchment firing, and salaries—a traditional practice that raised few hackles in the past.

What's caused the uproar is that the world is changing. America is moving from a national, analog, industrial economy to a global, digital, information economy. The two economies differ dramatically in their expectations for schools and teachers.

Industrial societies focus on common processes, epitomized by the assembly line. Our schools—products of the industrial age—rely on such processes: Schools enroll children at age 5, sort them into classes, teach them specified subjects for uniform lengths of time determined by the Carnegie Foundation for the Advancement of Teaching in 1906, and require attendance 180 days annually for 13 years. The focus is on teaching.

In contrast, information economies focus on common outcomes. Process is variable. With regard to schools, the emphasis is on learning; the question is whether students have mastered knowledge and skills, regardless of where, when, or how.

In the industrial-era school, the currency of education is time—how long students are taught. The assumption is that all students can learn the same things in the same period of time. In the information-era school, the currency is student achievement, and time is variable.

Unions and the Industrial Era

Herein lies the cause of current conflicts with teachers' unions. They, like schools, are products of the industrial era. They embrace the focus on teaching and advocate time-based rewards to teachers. Salary increases and pensions are based on longevity. Tenure is granted most commonly after three years. Pensions balloon for teachers who spend full careers teaching. Teachers with greater seniority can take the jobs of teachers with less seniority. The last hired teacher must be the first fired in a retrenchment. Given previous expectations for schools and teachers, these were logical practices, and unions have continued to support them.

Many policy makers, however, have adopted the information economy's focus on learning. Accordingly, they seek to overthrow the hegemony of time, recognizing that not all students learn the same amount in fixed time periods. Instead, they propose policies tied to educational outcomes: state standards for what students must learn; testing that assesses student progress toward the standards; test score–based evaluation of teacher performance in advancing student learning; and salary structures that link teachers' compensation to success in promoting student achievement. This agenda flies in the face of historic union policies and is diametrically opposed to an education system in which the currency is time and teaching.

The real problem, then, is not the individual issues that grab headlines. It is that, increasingly, policy makers and unions have fundamentally different visions of the work of schools and teachers. This is not to say unions have done something wrong. It's that the world changed around them. It is also important to note that the situation of teachers' unions is not unique. All of our social institutions—schools, government, media, health care, and finance—were created for an old-style industrial economy. All are out of date and appear to be broken. Each needs to be rethought for the present and the future. Government, so often critical of unions, has many of the same problems: vesting power on the basis of longevity, institutionalizing tenure through redistricting and opposition to term limits, focusing on process rather than outcomes, and engendering rising levels of public criticism.

In the years ahead, the burden will be on unions to develop policies rooted in information-era schools where student learning is the focus. They can play a vital role in building the information-age schools we need for tomorrow and in supporting the teachers those schools will require, or they will be viewed as obstructionist and ultimately become irrelevant. Some union leaders have already recognized the need for this shift, even as they perform a complicated balancing act, with one foot in the industrial era and one in the information era.

Still, the shift is inevitable. Unions can oppose it or lead the transition, preserving what history has shown to be essential while building the new that is needed. But first, they must understand, advocate, and embrace the seismic shift in how schools work.

| "The reason that public employee strikes are outlawed in all but 11 states has nothing to do with a threat to public safety. It's that governments are the only employers that actually have the ability to outlaw them."

Teachers and Public Employees Have the Right to Strike

Michael Hiltzik

Michael Hiltzik is a reporter for the Los Angeles Times. *In the following viewpoint, he argues that most public union strikes are not any more of a threat to public safety than other strikes. All strikes, he says, impose economic costs in an effort to improve workers' standing. Governments often outlaw public employee strikes because they can, and no employer likes strikes. However, a transit worker strike does not threaten public safety, as police and firefighter strikes might. Therefore, he concludes, public employees should have the right to strike.*

Michael Hiltzik, "Why Public Employees Should Have the Right to Strike," *Los Angeles Times*, October 24, 2013. Latimes.com. Copyright © 2013 Los Angeles Times. Reproduced by permission.

As you read, consider the following questions:

1. According to the viewpoint, who is Steve Glazer, and what argument did he make against the Bay Area Rapid Transit strike?

2. What evidence does Hiltzik offer that public employee strikes are rare?

3. Why do teachers and nurses have the best success in appealing to the public during strikes, in Hiltzik's view?

It would take a finely tuned instrument to measure the speed with which a strike by public employees is followed by politicians calling for a ban on this fundamental right of organized labor. Sure enough, the ink wasn't dry on the settlement ending the recent [2013] strike by workers for the Bay Area Rapid Transit [BART] system when a candidate for the State Assembly spoke up.

An Economic Threat

He's Steve Glazer, a Democrat running for a seat in the East Bay. "Transit is an essential public service, just like police and fire," he says. He argues that since California bans strikes by police and firefighters, transit strikes should be banned, too.

That's baloney. Glazer should just admit that he's pandering to the voters—he's been haunting BART stations to collect signatures for a petition to ban transit strikes—and stop trying to dress up his position as a matter of principle.

It's worth taking a quick look at the history of public employee strikes and how they compare to strikes in the private sector. Only 11 states allow any public employees to strike, and most of those impose limits. The most common restriction is a ban on strikes by police and firefighters, for the perfectly legitimate reason that those walkouts pose an immediate threat to public safety. But is that true of strikes by teachers, transit workers, DMV [Department of Motor Vehicles] clerks, park rangers, or almost any other category of public worker? Their walkouts pose an *economic* threat, which is very different. In fact, economic threats are the very essence of a strike. After all, if labor walkouts didn't impose hardship on the other side or on third parties like customers, who can themselves exert pressure for a settlement, there'd be no point to striking at all.

The reason that public employee strikes are outlawed in all but 11 states has nothing to do with a threat to public safety. It's that governments are the only employers that actually have the ability to outlaw them. There isn't an employer in the world who, given the authority, wouldn't do the same (and cook up a threadbare rationale for how strikes in this industry would compromise public safety). Supermarket owners? Airlines? UPS [United Parcel Service]? They'd all love to make strikes by their workers illegal. They just don't have the power.

That said, public employee strikes even in those 11 states are rare. As Melissa Maynard observed in the Pew Charitable Trusts' publication *Stateline*, last year's Chicago teachers strike, the most high-profile public employee walkout in recent years, was the first teachers strike in that city in 25 years and the first in a major city since a Detroit teachers strike in 2006.

The reason for the scarcity of public worker strikes has a lot to do with the dynamics of strikes in general. Employers and employees in any job action are making a calculation based on comparative hardship. Both sides sustain economic losses—the workers go without paychecks and risk losing their jobs, the employers lose income and risk losing customers, sometimes permanently. The goal is to survive the short-term economic loss while imposing greater costs on the other side, until one side or the other cries uncle.

Taxpayers (Usually) Hate Strikes

And both sides try to enlist the sympathy and support of customers. Teamsters [referring to the International Brotherhood

Right to Strike for Public Employees

From the historical aversion to the strike in the public sector and heavy reliance on mediation and fact-finding as substitute mechanisms, public policy makers have come to accept—though modestly—the limited right to strike as the mechanism to bring finality in bargaining short of an employer's unilateral action or an illegal employees strike. Under most statutes, state and local government employees are specifically prohibited from striking, but fourteen states now permit strikes by some government employees under certain circumstances, with certain strikes not allowed. Typically, the laws divide government employees into categories on the basis of whether the services they provide are "essential." Government employees who provide essential services are rarely, if ever, permitted to strike. A strike that threatens the public health, safety, and/or welfare triggers a "no-strike" mechanism. Where employees may strike, impasse procedures must typically be complied with. In some cases, essential employees not permitted to strike are provided compulsory arbitration of bargaining impasses.

In the federal sector the law prohibits strikes by government employees, unless the strikes are explicitly authorized by statute. Federal government employees who participate in a strike are permanently barred from federal employment and are guilty of a felony.

Joyce M. Najita and James L. Stern,
Collective Bargaining in the Public Sector:
The Experience of Eight States. *New York: Routledge, 2015.*

of Teamsters labor union] won a huge victory over UPS in a 15-day walkout in 1997, for example, because customers appreciated the efficiency of their UPS drivers, and management looked cheap and greedy. That's harder for public employees to achieve, in part because their customers, the taxpayers, also see themselves as their employers. And employers always hate strikes.

But it's not impossible. Teachers and public hospital nurses tend to have the greatest success, because often they can make the case that the services they provide are compromised by skinflint and inefficient management. Ask Arnold Schwarzenegger how his campaign against nurses turned out in 2006, when he tried to cut nurse staffing ratios in state hospitals. On the other hand, BART drivers didn't seem to have the public foursquare on their side in the recent job action. (That's not even counting the contempt shown to BART drivers by some overprivileged high-tech poohbahs.)

But there's no basis for the claim that public employee strikes, outside police and fire services, are uniquely dangerous or injurious to the community. Candidate Glazer complains that the BART strike forced commuters to find other means of getting to work or kept them home, hobbling the local economy. Yes, that's right. The same thing would have happened if the transit system were privately run, as it is in some places.

And strikes in any number of other private-sector industries also hobble the local economy and impose hardships on some people. Milk strikes. Truck driver strikes. Telephone lineman strikes. Port strikes. Fast-food worker strikes. The point in every case is not to minimize or moderate the impact, but try to stick the other side with the blame. And in that, public employees deserve no less the right than the rest of us to give it a shot.

> *"The long attempt to stem the decline in education standards has been blocked at every turn by the teaching unions, who appear to be in business to perpetuate mediocrity and protect the incompetent."*

Teachers Have a Duty of Care to Their Pupils and That Is Why They Should Never Go on Strike

Melanie Phillips

Melanie Phillips is a British journalist who has written for the Guardian, *the* Daily Mail, *the* Times, *and other publications. In the following viewpoint, she argues that teachers have a duty of care to students and should therefore never be allowed to strike. She adds that teachers have resisted tough standards for students, resulting in a dumbed-down curriculum that shortchanges pupils. She concludes that teachers have broadly failed students and that thoroughgoing educational reform is needed.*

Melanie Phillips, "Teachers Have a Duty of Care to Their Pupils and That Is Why They Should Never Go on Strike," *Daily Mail*, June 27, 2011. Dailymail.co.uk. Copyright © 2011 Associated Newspapers Ltd. Reproduced by permission.

As you read, consider the following questions:

1. According to the viewpoint, what did Education Secretary Michael Gove recommend parents do while teachers are on strike?

2. According to Phillips, what is the "appalling reality" that has led to less rigorous teacher standards?

3. Who does Phillips believe will be most affected by the failure of schools?

Sometimes, going on strike is the last refuge of the useless. This Thursday, more than 100,000 teachers are mounting a one-day strike in a dispute over changes to their pensions.

In response, the Education Secretary Michael Gove has taken an uncompromising line in urging parents to break the strike by coming into school and taking lessons themselves.

The response by the education unions co-ordinating this strike—the National Union of Teachers (NUT) and the Association of Teachers and Lecturers (ATL)—has been to issue lame warnings that any such parents will fall foul of health-and-safety rules.

The harm the striking teachers will cause children by disrupting their education is, of course, not acknowledged.

Now we learn in addition that those organising these strikes are little more than activists whose anti-social activities are actually subsidised from the public purse.

Although some don't teach at all, or work in schools only part-time, these union organisers are paid by local councils to the tune of £15.1 million per year.

And to rub salt into the wound, Christine Blower, the leader of the NUT, is pocketing a 10 per cent pay rise—twice the rate of inflation—as she prepares to lead her members out on strike.

There is an overwhelming argument for saying teachers should never strike because of the damage it does to children's interests.

After all, teaching is much more than a mere job. It is a vocation, which necessarily entails a duty of care towards the pupils of whose once-in-a-lifetime education teachers are the custodians.

For sure, there are many fine and committed teachers who do indeed understand what education is all about.

And there are even more who do the very best they can for the pupils they teach—and who all too often have to suffer an escalating tide of disruptive behaviour, aggression and violence not just from pupils but from their parents.

But the awful fact is that the guts were ripped out of teaching long ago.

From the seventies onwards, state education stopped being about the transmission of knowledge. Ludicrous ideological fads inimical to education took over instead.

Educationalists decided children should learn not from teachers but from their own experience. Any kind of structured teaching was regarded as an assault upon a child's autonomy and a threat to his or her self-esteem.

Teachers accordingly took a back seat as mere 'facilitators' of a child's voyage of discovery. Not surprisingly, abandoning children to make their own way through the world without the intellectual maps to guide them resulted in children learning very little at all.

Some of those children went on to become teachers themselves. And so an alarming proportion of today's teachers don't even have the knowledge they need to pass on to their pupils—even if they wanted to.

Now, teacher-training institutions are apparently to set tougher entrance requirements to ensure that trainee teachers have mastered basic literacy and numeracy.

Alas, we have been here before. This requirement was introduced many years ago.

But the appalling reality was that so many candidates failed to reach this elementary standard that insisting it was met would have meant there weren't enough teachers being trained.

Thus, it was watered down so candidates didn't have to pass these literacy or numeracy tests before being accepted into teacher training.

Currently, they can take as many re-sits as they need. Now this is about to change. The education secretary is reportedly publishing new requirements this week which will allow only two re-sits of these 'basic skills' tests.

But even if this higher hurdle survives, we're not exactly talking pedagogic polymaths here: The standard of these tests for teachers is said to be more suited to primary schoolchildren.

It tells you everything you need to know about the dire state of education in Britain that standards are to be raised by allowing trainee teachers three attempts only (!) to spell 'mathematical', for example, or to add up three times 24 and four times 28.

The disdain for transmitting knowledge and the resulting collapse of teaching are the core reasons why education standards have gone down the pan.

Last week, Sir Terry Leahy, the former chief executive of Tesco, became the latest in a string of industrialists and business leaders who have warned that poor standards in schools and universities leave young people ill-prepared for work.

More pupils, said Sir Terry, need to be taught 'harder' subjects at school, such as mathematics, sciences and languages.

If only! The problem is that so many teachers and educationalists just don't agree with him. Or if they appear to do so, what they are actually agreeing to teach is such a dumbed-down version of maths, science or languages as to make a mockery of education.

"I WAS PRO-UNION WHEN I WAS A KID, AND THE TEACHERS WERE ON STRIKE."

© Jack Corbett, "I was pro-union when I was a kid, and the teachers were on strike ...," CartoonStock.com.

The education establishment has managed to undermine all attempts to stop the rot.

In a programme for BBC Radio 4, the broadcaster John Humphrys discovered that after the Welsh abolished school SATs and league tables, exam performance in Wales declined by no less than an estimated two GCSE grades per pupil.

According to the Programme for International Student Assessment, which looks at education systems worldwide, the Welsh are now well below the average for the developed world for reading and even lower for maths.

When Humphrys returned to his old primary school in Cardiff, he found there was no structured literacy or numeracy hour. Instead, the children weren't so much being taught as 'learning by doing'—which the rest of us would call playing—and could do pretty much what they liked.

Charitably (or perhaps naively), Humphrys seemed prepared to believe that such an approach could work. But at one Cardiff secondary school, he found that only 16 per cent of the children could read properly, and some had the reading age of a four-year-old.

Well, this is where many of us came in more than two decades ago, when the [Margaret] Thatcher government belatedly realised British education standards were in free fall precisely because of this 'child-centred' approach.

Allowing children effectively to teach themselves most certainly does not work. It leaves children stranded in ignorance and unable to think.

And the worst affected are those from the poorest households, for whom school is their one ladder of opportunity.

This ladder has been kicked away from underneath them by an educational orthodoxy which has substituted jargon for knowledge and gobbledegook for academic rigour.

The Conservative government tried to address this catastrophe through the National Curriculum, SATs and national literacy and numeracy programmes.

But the National Curriculum was subverted from the start. Teachers resisted tooth and nail every attempt to get them to teach children to read by the one tried-and-tested system of structured phonics.

As for SATs, these were regularly manipulated to give the false impression of rising standards.

So we're more or less back where we started, and Mr Gove has a truly Sisyphean task.

The long attempt to stem the decline in education standards has been blocked at every turn by the teaching unions, who appear to be in business to perpetuate mediocrity and protect the incompetent.

Mr Gove's provocative call to parents to break the strike may have incensed the teachers. But it is their own proposed militancy this week that is a step too far.

Periodical and Internet Sources Bibliography

The following articles have been selected to supplement the diverse views presented in this chapter.

Dave Chase	"Teacher Unions on Wrong Side of Negotiating Table," *Forbes*, June 12, 2015.
Amy B. Dean	"Protecting Classrooms from Corporate Take-over: What Families Can Learn from Teachers' Unions," *Yes!*, April 18, 2014.
Emily Ekins	"Polling Shows Most Americans Think Teachers Unions Have Hurt Public Education Quality," *Reason*, September 10, 2012.
Diana Furchtgott-Roth and Jared Meyer	"Teachers' Unions Throw Students Under the Bus," Real Clear Markets, May 7, 2015.
Rob Furman	"Unions—Good or Bad for Education?," *Huffington Post*, October 4, 2012.
Douglas Hodum	"The Biggest Misconceptions About Teachers' Unions—Debunked," TakePart, May 28, 2015.
James Paul	"Our Undemocratic Teachers' Unions," *National Review*, March 25, 2015.
Caroline Porter and Melanie Trottman	"Teachers Unions Under Fire," *Wall Street Journal*, September 4, 2014.
Gary Raviani	"Why Public Education Needs Teachers Unions," EdSource, July 27, 2014.
Stephanie Simon	"The Fall of Teachers Unions," *Politico*, June 13, 2014.
Valerie Strauss	"How Teachers Unions Must Change—by a Union Leader," *Washington Post*, February 13, 2015.

CHAPTER 2

What Are Ethical Issues Surrounding Teachers' Working Conditions?

Chapter Preface

In the United States, many people who can afford to do so send their children to private schools rather than to public schools. This may be for religious, educational, or social reasons. Generally, parents who use private schools believe that those schools are better for their children.

Some writers, such as Allison Benedikt of *Slate*, however, have argued that sending a child to private school is an unethical decision. "You are a bad person if you send your children to private school," Benedikt insists. "Not bad like *murderer* bad—but bad like *ruining-one-of-our-nation's-most-essential-institutions-in-order-to-get-what's-best-for-your-kid* bad. So, pretty bad."

Benedikt's point is that public schools need the support of all families if they are to thrive. When families with the most resources, knowledge, and connections abandon the public schools, public schools are weakened, creating a two-tier system of rich and poor schools. "Everyone needs to be invested in our public schools in order for them to get better. Not just lip service investment or property tax investment, but real flesh-and-blood-offspring investment," Benedikt argues.

Many writers disagree with Benedikt. However, one issue that is less discussed is the ethical duty of teachers. If private schools are unethical, does that mean that teachers who teach at those schools are immoral?

This question raises another: Why do teachers teach at private schools? Average salaries in public schools are $50,000 a year; average salaries in private schools are $36,000 a year. That is an enormous gap. So why would anyone want to be a private school teacher?

The reasons are numerous. First, public schools often require more schooling, or more accreditation to teach. In other words, many private school teachers cannot teach in public schools without returning to school themselves.

Beyond that, though, as Ben Orlin writes in the *Atlantic*, private schools are often much better places to work than public ones. "Class sizes are smaller—a 12:1 student-to-teacher ratio, compared with 16:1 at public schools. There's also less red tape—private teachers answer to principals and parents, rather than to principals, parents, and three meddling levels of government." Private schools allow teachers to teach with less bureaucratic interference. That's a major incentive.

Teachers, then, may want to teach at private schools for ethical reasons. They may feel that at private schools they can do their jobs better or focus more on the parts of the job they think are important. Is it ethically wrong to want to do the best job possible? What ethical duty do teachers owe to their students, and what ethical duty do they owe to society as a whole? The following chapter examines these questions in the context of charter schools, district schools, and programs such as Teach For America.

> "*[Teach For America] undermines the American public education system . . . by urging the replacement of experienced career teachers with a neoliberal model of interchangeable educators and standardized testing.*"

Teach For America Is Unethical

Sandra Y.L. Korn

Sandra Y.L. Korn is a former Harvard Crimson *editorial writer and an analyst at the Croatan Institute for social and economic research. In the following viewpoint, she argues that Teach For America teachers are unprepared to enter classrooms and educate students. She also says that Teach For America is used to take jobs from veteran teachers, damage neighborhood schools in favor of charters, and generally undermine the voices of teachers, children, and neighborhoods in education. She concludes that it is unethical to teach for Teach For America, and she suggests that Teach For America volunteers should rethink their commitments.*

Sandra Y.L. Korn, "Don't Teach For America," *Harvard Crimson*, October 23, 2013. Thecrimson.com. Copyright © 2013 The Harvard Crimson. Reproduced by permission.

As you read, consider the following questions:

1. What is the first reason Korn gives for not wanting to be a Teach For America teacher?

2. What evidence does Korn cite to show that Teach For America is hurting teachers and schools in Chicago?

3. To what has Teach For America positioned itself as an ethical alternative, according to Korn?

Last month [in September 2013], I got an email from a recruiter. An associate of Teach For America [TFA], citing a minor leadership role in a student organization as evidence that I "have distinguished [myself] as a leader here on Harvard's campus," asked me to meet with Harvard's TFA representative on campus. Dropping phrases like "race and class," "equal opportunities," and "educational injustice," the recruiter promised that I could have a significant impact on a classroom in an underserved community.

Not Ready to Enter a Classroom

I have thought for many years about teaching high school history. But I stopped replying to this email after a few exchanges.

I am not interested in TFA.

For one, I am far from ready to enter a classroom on my own. Indeed, in my experience Harvard students have increasingly acknowledged that TFA drastically underprepares its recruits for the reality of teaching. But more importantly, TFA is not only sending young, idealistic, and inexperienced college grads into schools in neighborhoods different from where they're from—it's also working to destroy the American public education system. As a hopeful future teacher, that is not something I could ever conscionably put my name behind.

Princeton alumna Wendy Kopp originally founded TFA with the mission of filling teacher shortages in U.S. public schools. The program, which helps young college grads find placements teaching in public schools after they graduate from college, combines the persistence of a five-person recruiting team with the cache of a competitive on-campus interview process. It has quickly become one of the most popular destinations for Harvard seniors after graduation.

Clearly, some Harvard students still believe that TFA's model of recruiting young idealists, throwing them into five weeks of intensive training, and then placing them into schools in neighborhoods very unlike the ones they came from is truly the answer to everything from income inequality to underfunded public school systems. Perhaps they even think that teaching is such an unattractive profession that bright college graduates should be bribed with a feel-good résumé booster to fill the vast shortage of competent teachers in the United States.

But it has become increasingly clear to anyone who thinks critically about teaching that there's something off with TFA's model. After all, TFA alumni repeatedly describe their stints in the American public education system as some of the hardest two years of their lives. Doesn't it bother you to imagine undertrained 22-year-olds standing in front of a crowded classroom and struggling through every class period? Indeed, most of the critiques of TFA in the *Crimson* have focused on students' unpreparedness to teach.

Undermining Public Education

However, unpreparedness pales in comparison to the much larger problem with TFA: It undermines the American public education system from the very foundation by urging the replacement of experienced career teachers with a neoliberal model of interchangeable educators and standardized testing. If TFA intended to place students in schools with insufficient numbers of teachers, it has strayed far from its original goal. As an essay by Chicago teacher Kenzo Shibata asked last summer, "Teach For America wanted to help stem a teacher short-

Teach For America Controversy

Teach For America [TFA] teachers became some of the most scrutinized workers in the nation, with researchers tracking their career trajectories, their attitudes about politics and society, and their students' test scores. The debate TFA opened up about teacher preparation and quality teaching, while often rancorous, has been deeper and more evidence based than any the nation has had since the inception of common schooling in the nineteenth century. In part, this is because so many TFA alumni have written frankly about their experiences. . . .

Jonathan Schorr was one early critic from within the TFA family. After sixteen years of private schooling, including college at Yale, Schorr sailed through his TFA summer institute student teaching, in which he was responsible for a group of only four students. He entered his classroom at Pasadena High School with naïve enthusiasm. But as the newest teacher, Schorr was assigned the toughest students, and he found himself trying, and often failing, to reach a group of kids who included teen parents and students with severe disabilities, behavior problems, and legal troubles. "Giving the least experienced teachers the toughest classes to teach is a stupid plan, even for the most eager of teachers," Schorr concluded in a widely cited 1993 *Phi Delta Kappan* article. "Though I would not have admitted it at the time, I—perhaps like most TFAers—harbored dreams of liberating my students from public school mediocrity and offering them as good an education as I had received. But I was not ready."

Dana Goldstein,
The Teacher Wars: A History of America's Most
Embattled Profession. *New York: Random House, 2014.*

age. Why then are thousands of experienced educators being replaced by hundreds of new college graduates?" Journalist James Cersonsky notes that veteran teachers and schools alike may suffer from this type of reform: "Districts pay thousands in fees to TFA for each corps member in addition to their salaries—at the expense of the existing teacher workforce. Chicago, for example, is closing 48 schools and laying off 850 teachers and staff while welcoming 350 corps members."

Chicago is not the first city where Teach For America has tried to replace veteran teachers with new recruits. Two years ago, the *Crimson* quoted the president of the Boston Teachers Union as saying, "Teach For America claims that it does not come in and take positions from incumbent members. That is a lie. They are doing it in Boston. . . . Their arrogance is appalling." Cersonsky and blogger EduShyster have meticulously documented TFA's connections to dozens of charter schools as well as education reform advocacy organizations that focus on standardized testing and privatization instead of grassroots community involvement and student voices. In doing so, TFA is working directly against the interests of teachers, students, and communities alike. Neoliberal school reform is the true "educational injustice" here.

Happily, Chicago does provide a model of truly community-driven and progressive education advocacy. Last summer, the Chicago Teachers Union organized with parents and students to advocate for quality public education including smaller class sizes, more staff-like school nurses, less standardized testing, and progressive taxation structures for school funding.

I don't mean to vilify students who've chosen to recruit for TFA—I'm sure they have only the best intentions of helping underserved students—but I would like to call on my classmates and current TFA corps members to reconsider their decision to be part of this program. TFA has positioned itself as an ethical alternative to Wall Street for college seniors looking for a short-term commitment. We should all have questions about how much we can actually help to fix structural problems with just a month of training and a few years of work.

> *"If we think clearly about what adjunct professors do, we will realize that they are skilled contract labor, who usually get paid a fairly high hourly rate to deliver a concise service."*

Treatment of College Adjunct Professors Is Ethical

Eric Charles

Eric Charles runs the research lab at the Center for Teaching, Research & Learning at American University. In the following viewpoint, he argues that adjunct professors are highly skilled contractors who receive a high hourly rate without benefits. He says they are comparable to other highly skilled contractors, such as motivational speakers, and nothing is inherently unjust in the fact that they do not receive health benefits. He says adjuncts are sometimes poorly treated, but he says they are not hard laborers and that traditional unionization is not a good solution to their problems.

Eric Charles, PhD, "What's Wrong with (the Rhetoric Surrounding) Adjuncts?," *Psychology Today*, October 16, 2013. Psychologytoday.com. Copyright © 2013 Psychology Today. Reproduced by permission.

As you read, consider the following questions:

1. How have some used the story of the Duquesne adjunct to argue for unionization, according to Charles?

2. How much does Charles say an adjunct professor teaching first-year French might make?

3. What union did Charles join when he was in graduate school?

The adjuncts vs. professors conundrum has been on my mind. In a recent post, I talked about why it should be hard to compare what adjuncts bring to a classroom with what research-active professors bring to the classroom. I avoided the really tough talk in the last article, and I will avoid it here as well. However, I hope to lay some groundwork, inspired by a recent story.

Adjuncts Are Compensated Like Other Experts

The story involves a woman who died at 83, having taught French for 25 years at Duquesne University, in Pittsburgh, Pennsylvania. The context of the story, as usually presented, is that Duquesne is not letting its adjuncts unionize and, due to the lack of a union, the woman died without proper health care and nigh homeless. The details of the story are sketchy; as in, they are only loosely sketched out anywhere I have found them. Where were Social Security and Medicare? How does a college stop the organization of a well-mustered union? Etc.

All that aside . . . while I do not think I am a heartless troll, I have trouble fully sympathizing with those who feel that the woman should have been entitled to more from Duquesne than she received. The plights described in the sketched version of the woman's story are NOT unique to adjunct professors, it is a trait that many members of Expertland share.

Lawyers, statistical analysts, surgeons, and many other types of experts typically get paid for delivery of skills only, and the hourly rate they get paid is expected to cover preparation and training. For example, I recently had some great conversation with a motivational speaker who gets paid several thousand for an afternoon. That may seem like a lot, but he has spent decades perfecting his presentation, and he still spends at least a full week on each one, between preparatory work, travel, and takedown. He is hard-pressed to do more than three workshops a month, and that places him squarely in a non-extravagant salary band, despite the seemingly insane hourly rate.

Similarly, but on a lesser scale, an adjunct professor teaching first-year French might make $3,000 a course, which works out to about $50 an hour. Surely there is a lot of prep the adjunct has done throughout his or her life to prepare for these in-class moments, and the delivery is expected to reflect that. However, when push comes to shove, someone teaching one class is only working three or four hours a week for the college, six to eight if you include office hours. The rest of the time is equivalent to the prep and takedown routinely expected of other experts.

Adjuncts Are Not Factory Workers

So now some questions: If your business had a lawyer, or sign-language interpreter, or engineering consultant, who worked for six hours a week, would you give them health insurance? If you had someone giving your child piano lessons or French lessons for six hours a week, would you give them health insurance? Would it change if your kids were getting group lessons? What if they were older? To get back to the original issues: Why should it be different if you are a college that has someone teach two rooms of students, each for three hours per week? I'm not saying that this is the way the world should work, but I am saying that it is a situation in no way

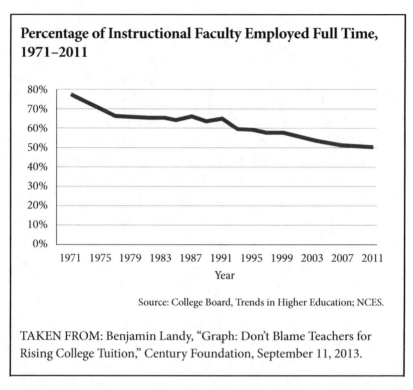

Percentage of Instructional Faculty Employed Full Time, 1971–2011

Year

Source: College Board, Trends in Higher Education; NCES.

TAKEN FROM: Benjamin Landy, "Graph: Don't Blame Teachers for Rising College Tuition," Century Foundation, September 11, 2013.

unique to academia, and that adjuncts are not in particularly more plight than any other expert who works as a part-time contractor. So, does the attitude of the college make sense? Yes. Are many adjunct professors being exploited? Yes, again. The problem is in the job itself. Many people doing the job are not the type of people the job was originally intended for. Unfortunately, the academic job market is so out of balance, and there is a mass of degree holders so myopic in their job seeking.... But I'm trying to put off the hard discussion for at least one more post....

The story that started this off was about adjunct professors trying to become steelworkers. When I was in graduate school at UC [University of California] Davis, similar processes led to my suddenly becoming an automotive worker—United Automotive Workers (UAW) 2865. The result was sad. The adjuncts I know do not want to be treated like members of a factory line. They don't want (as we received in graduate school) a quote of how many hours they are to spend grading every week, as if each week was the same. They don't want to be represented by people who see them as laborers and treat the rest of the college as management. Neither graduate students nor adjunct professors do jobs comparable to the groups these union organizations normally represent. Forming a dedicated adjunct union is not a bad idea, but making it so adjuncts are treated like factory-line workers won't help anything.

If we think clearly about what adjunct professors do, we will realize that they are skilled contract labor, who usually get paid a fairly high hourly rate to deliver a concise service. There are many dedicated adjuncts who deserve to be treated much better than they are treated. However, we are not helped by romanticized rhetoric that hides what the job actually is.

> "To be truly ahead of the game, the 'percentage of faculty who are full-time' should be front and center on the rankings list, before even student-to-faculty ratio."

Hit 'Em Where It Hurts

Rebecca Schuman

Rebecca Schuman is an education columnist for Slate. *In the following viewpoint, she argues that the use of adjunct professors delivers subpar education and that students and parents should know this information before enrolling in colleges. Schuman maintains that adjuncts are not afforded the same resources as full-time faculty members and as such are not able to provide students with the quality education they deserve. She calls upon* U.S. News & World Report *to track universities' use of adjunct professors and disclose that information in its rankings of the best colleges. This, Schuman says, would sway consumers' college selection and would force colleges to consider how adjuncts are treated.*

Rebecca Schuman, From *Slate Magazine*, January 30, 2014. © 2014 Slate Magazine. All rights reserved. Used by permission and protected by the Copyright Laws of the United States. The printing, copying, redistribution, or retransmission of this Content without express written permission is prohibited.

As you read, consider the following questions:

1. Why does Schuman say adjuncts deliver subpar education to students?

2. What data does Schuman say the *U.S. News* rankings offer?

3. According to Schuman, what percentage of contingent faculty does Ohio State University have?

Changes are afoot among us part-time adjuncts who shoulder a hefty majority of college instruction in the United States. We have, for now, the attention of Congress. We've got our own snappy hashtags! And we're methodically organizing ourselves into unions, in my town and yours. Administrations are noticing, and are none too pleased. Sometimes, they go to impressive lengths to prevent a vote. Other times, they just issue veiled threats, saying they're "concerned" about faculty "ceding their individual right[s]" to the Service Employees International Union, an "outside organization" unfamiliar, "in all frankness," with "the enterprise of higher education."

Nice adjunct job you got there—it would be a shame if you didn't exercise your right to self-determination, and something happened to it. But that's just it: Adjunct jobs *aren't* nice, and many of us feel, in all frankness, that we have little to lose. But sympathy for the adjunct's plight is limited. (Read any comments section, ever, on any article with the word "adjunct" in it.) We *chose*, after all, to devote our lives to something so stupid and useless. Supply and demand. *Find another job.* Bootstraps. I get it.

But here's what *they* don't get: It's not that adjuncts deserve better. It's that students deserve better than adjuncts. And the people who decide which colleges are the "best" should be telling you this, but they're not. That's why I'm calling on *U.S. News*, the leading college ranking service in the country, to track the percentage of classes taught by adjuncts in their rankings—and penalize schools that use too many.

Here's the cold, hard truth every prospective student, and every parent, should know: In the vast majority of subjects, when you have an adjunct professor instead of a full-timer, *you are getting a substandard education.* To say this, I am admitting that I myself provide subpar service to my students. But I do.

I'm not subpar on purpose—I, like most adjuncts, just don't have the resources to treat students well. Like, you know, my own office, where I can meet with students when *they're* free, instead of the tiny weekly window of time when I get the desk and computer (which runs Windows XP) to myself. I am on campus five hours a week, because when I'm not in the classroom, I have nowhere else to go. If my students need further explanation, they can talk to me in class, or they can wait for whatever terse, harried lines I email them back (*if* I do; with all the jobs I juggle, sometimes I forget). I teach the same freshman survey over and over again, so I rarely have a student more than once, and thus never build a mentoring relationship with anyone. I am, by virtue of the parameters of my position, not giving students anything *remotely* near their money's worth. And hundreds of thousands of adjuncts in the United States are just like me. Most of those adjuncts would be giving their students a much better education, were they only provided the support that a college gives its full-time faculty. But they aren't, and the effect on student learning is—surprise—deleterious.

As much as I support efforts to mobilize and unionize, we also need a different tactic. Today's students view themselves as customers, and college as an excruciatingly expensive service. Most humanists balk at this crass, Randian characterization, but not me. I cleave onto it wholeheartedly, because it is in the revelation of the poor "service" adjuncts provide that we might finally hit universities where it hurts: *their rankings.*

Institutions, no matter what they say, are mortally invested in their placement on the *U.S. News* Best Colleges list. But although the freely available rankings share data about endowment, SAT scores, class size, and student-to-faculty ratio, they do not list percentage of part-time faculty. That does not mean the ranking metric doesn't include this data, explained Robert J. Morse, *U.S. News'* director of research data. Morse assured me *U.S. News* is actually "far ahead of the game" on holding institutions who overuse part-time faculty accountable, because in their ranking factor, "schools get more credit for a larger proportion of full-time faculty." He explained that schools who use a large portion of part-time faculty "score lower" on the ranking metric, but wouldn't specify how much lower. Is overuse of part-time faculty as bad as a meager endowment? Worse than lackluster SAT scores? It really should be. (If you'd like to do the math yourself, here's the *U.S. News* formula for 2014; proportion of full-time faculty makes up 5 percent of the "faculty resources" indicator, which itself makes up 20 percent of the ranking model.)*

To be truly ahead of the game, the "percentage of faculty who are full-time" should be front and center on the rankings list, before even student-to-faculty ratio. Instead, it's tucked away inside the paid version of *U.S. News'* ranking website, so most "education consumers" will never see it—even though it should be the *first* thing you ask when you and your kid are touring a campus. Whether or not some sports nut who graduated in 1952 gives bank to the football team should matter much, much less than whether or not your professor has slept in a heated house, and thus prepared your lesson effectively.

U.S. News and its ilk must enjoy the power they have over these hapless institutions—so they ought to wield that power for good. Don't just factor in the use (and overuse) of part-time faculty, but *all* contingent faculty. *Destroy the standing* of any institution that does not have a sizeable majority of fac-

Commodification of Professors

In an essay titled "First Year Commodity: The Adjunct Professor Labor Crisis in Composition Departments," Josh Boldt, the founder of the Adjunct Project, . . . sums up the way adjuncts develop from and depend on commodification and how the students at these schools suffer as well from the phenomenon:

> The new career track for university faculty is that of the Disposable Professor. As we rely more and more on adjunct professor labor, we slowly surrender our power on college campuses. Contingent faculty are, by definition, powerless. Completely replaceable. No tenure, no bargaining rights, no contract, no voice. First-year composition departments are all too familiar with this reality, as they are staffed predominantly by non-tenure-track, contingent faculty. Adjuncts, and therefore the composition department they staff, are powerless in the economic equation of the "corporatized" university.

He gives us unsettling numbers of how elsewhere commodification affects our educational system. Reminding us that 70 percent of America's teaching faculty hold adjunct positions, he writes, "This ratio has skyrocketed by 280 percent in the past 30 years. . . . And each year it's only getting worse. Non-tenure-track appointments have climbed 7.6 percent in the past three years alone. At this rate, it's only a matter of time before 'college professor' is no longer a viable profession."

James F. Keenan, University Ethics:
How Colleges Can Build and Benefit from a Culture of Ethics.
Lanham, MD: Rowman & Littlefield, 2015.

ulty that are full-time, preferably tenure-track or tenured. Or, at the very least, list the institution's percentages front and center, with an explanation of why this factor is so crucial in choosing a college. Because this information is not forthcoming on most university websites—and you can see why, when organizations such as the Ohio Part-Time Faculty Association report that my former employer, the "public Ivy" Ohio State, has 65 *percent contingent faculty.* And yet it's still ranked on *U.S. News* as the No. 52 national university in the country. Why? With a percentage like that, it shouldn't even be in the double digits, no matter how much wealthy former Buckeyes donate.

If a college or university's ranking—and concurrently, as others are calling for, even its accreditation—could be *openly* and seriously damaged by the overuse of contingent faculty, then and only then would students and parents actually begin to care, and they'd vote with their tuition. And then and only then would administrations actually begin to . . . well, "care" isn't the right word. Let's say they'd finally find something about contingent faculty to be *concerned* about, other than the union.

*Correction: This article misstated that U.S. News' ranking metric is private; the magazine published its 2014 formula here [http://www.usnews.com/education/best-colleges/articles/how-us-news-calculated-the-rankings].

> *"Every June 1, the exhausted teachers and staff at my school learn whether they will be rehired for another grueling year."*

A Teacher's Perspective: Firing Day at a Charter School

Nancy Bloom

Nancy Bloom is a former teacher at a charter school. In the following viewpoint, she says that working conditions in the charter school in which she was employed were unpleasant and disrespectful. Teachers were expected to work long hours for little pay, and administrators laughed and gloated that conditions were worse than in public schools. She maintains that in charter schools, some teachers are arbitrarily fired after the school year, with little notice and often too late to find other jobs. Bloom says that teachers' unions at least prevent such arbitrary decisions and force administration to treat teachers with some consideration.

Nancy Bloom, "A Teacher's Perspective: Firing Day at a Charter School," *CoLab Radio*, May 31, 2012. colabradio.mit.edu. Copyright © 2012 Community Innovators Lab. Reproduced by permission.

As you read, consider the following questions:

1. According to the viewpoint, how many teachers were fired the year before Bloom quit, and which one does she name specifically?

2. Why does Bloom believe that the administration keeps the firings secret until the last moment?

3. What caused Bloom to know she had to quit?

I just quit my job as a teacher in an urban charter school. Even though I still don't have another job and I support myself entirely, it is the best decision I ever made. It is especially liberating this week while my colleagues—and after five incredibly stressful years on the education front lines, my truly beloved friends—wait for the June 1 ax to fall.

Every June 1, the exhausted teachers and staff at my school learn whether they will be rehired for another grueling year. Last year the school gave 43 staff and teachers the you're-outta-luck-pal letters, including the entire three-man physical education department and the student support genius, Dany Edwards, who somehow made harmony out of the school's cacophony of crazy student behavior. This year the school's three glorious new gymnasiums are largely unused because we have no gym teachers, and Dany is dead of unknown causes. Whatever happened to this beautiful young man, firing him didn't help him live any better or happier for his last few months on earth. And the kids he championed lost his tender, tough, hilarious and real guidance.

This post is dedicated to you Dany, one year after you ran from the building in frantic disbelief, waving your letter as you ran up and down Hyde Park Avenue, looking for people to share your grief. If they can fire you, they can fire any of us. Except they can't fire me. I beat them at their game.

The first thing you need to know reader, is that there is no job security at a charter school. Even excellent veteran educators, like the three physical education teachers who were fired one year ago, are vulnerable. Between them, these men gave something like 35 years to the school. They offered serious nutrition education in their fight against childhood obesity. They miraculously coached kids who have hair-trigger tempers through team sports without breakout fights. They taught the kids good sportsmanship and how to represent themselves, their families and the school during games at other schools. They taught yoga, which the kids actually used to calm themselves in class. And they worked the kids hard. Oh how I miss seeing the kids come to class from gym all red and sweaty and happy. This gymless year, the kids seem fatter and more out of breath as they huff and puff their way to the third floor.

To you Michelle Rhee and all you antiunion fanatics, you are wasting your time waiting around for superman. They already fired superman at my school. You see a union would have protected Dany as well as these three talented teachers who provided quality physical education to all of our 1200 students. Meanwhile, some not-so-gifted staff and teachers get to keep their jobs every June 1. At least public schools and their unions have transparent guidelines for tenure and enough respect to let teachers know they won't be rehired for the next school year by March or earlier. June 1 is late to jump into the teacher hiring season. I suspect the administration keeps it a secret to the bitter end because they don't trust us to keep working hard. They are suspicious and we are paranoid. It's part of my school's culture.

The second thing to know is that we work very hard at my charter school, completing endless tasks that are not designed to instill habits of critical thinking in our students. Rather we are driven like cattle to collect mounds of data, to divvy the data up into tidy and irrelevant skill categories, and finally to create individual action plans to remediate each student's poor data points. We are required to write lesson plans that note exactly which discrete skills we will be working on during every minute of every school day while delivering scripted programs. It takes hours to make these plans, and we don't use them. Can't use them. Because kids are unpredictable and surprises happen. Most of us work at least ten hours on every weekday preparing our rooms and teaching. We continue working on weekends. The building is open on Saturdays and during vacations, and there are a lot of cars in the parking lot on these days off.

This heavy workload doesn't even take into account the trauma and anguish of working with urban children who suffer all the indignities of poverty. One day last week I had to file three mental health emergencies for neglect—two for kids who reeked of urine and one for a boy who was wobbly with hunger. One of our school psychologists once explained that many of our students come to school afraid and then stay afraid all day, afraid that their home or family may not be there when they get off the bus. These are the kids who constantly disrupt the classrooms. If Dany had been allowed to continue his ministerial work, he would still be providing discipline, safety and love for these broken children. And he would be giving us teachers rock-solid support without judgement in our struggle to keep these kids learning. The school psychologist said she prayed for the students' safety every night. In case you are wondering, she quit before they got a chance to fire her.

Our workload is a favorite theme of the school's superintendent and CEO. Charter school leaders love these business-style titles. Dr. CEO often chuckles during all-staff meetings at how we charter school teachers work harder than they do in Boston Public Schools and get paid less for our troubles. Apparently he doesn't know how insulting this is. Last December a group of administrators entertained us during a holiday party with a school version of "'Twas the Night Before Christmas" that included a verse about how little we get paid for our hefty workload. That was the last time I worked a ten-hour day and the moment I knew I had to quit.

The third and last thing for you to know is that psychological torture precedes the June 1 firing ritual in the form of annual performance reviews. It looks like our new principal has brought this final blow to a new level. I've talked to many teachers, and they report the same experience. He begins the review with gracious smiles and copious thank-yous for our commitment and hard work. And then he trashes our performance. So many of us have "failed to meet professional standards," you would think the school could barely function. Teachers are leaving their performance reviews convinced their June 1 letter will be very bad news. They have to sweat it out to June 1.

The most disturbing part is that the principal already knows who will be rehired. And he knows which teachers have especially compelling reasons to stay one more year. But he keeps them guessing. He doesn't even give them a reassuring wink or a thumbs up. Just a fake thank-you. Another administrator asked me last week if people were freaking out and then changed our plans for getting a drink after work on June 1. "I don't want to be out when people are all upset about losing their jobs."

This week it feels like the school's windows have been draped with heavy black curtains and the fluorescent ceiling lights are flickering. The kids are more difficult than ever, and we don't have Dany to let the sunlight in. No matter what happens Dany, I will never work in another charter school. That's the least I could do.

> "It's impossible to pretend that the number of firings actually reflects the number of bad teachers protected by tenure."

Tenure Protects High School Teachers Who Should Be Fired

Teachers Union Exposed

Teachers Union Exposed is a special project of the Center for Union Facts, a nonprofit organization dedicated to exposing the problems with teachers' unions. In the following viewpoint, the organization argues that very few teachers are fired, even in school districts with poor graduation rates and low test scores. The organization blames tenure, which teachers receive usually after only a few years and which makes them nearly impossible to fire. Teachers Union Exposed concludes that tenure keeps bad teachers in the classroom and harms students who deserve competent teachers.

As you read, consider the following questions:

1. How has tenure changed from its original intent, in the author's view?

"Protecting Bad Teachers," Teachers Union Exposed, n.d. Teachersunionexposed.com. Copyright © Teachers Union Exposed. Reproduced by permission.

2. According to the viewpoint, how many teachers have been fired in New Jersey's school system?

3. What did Michelle Rhee propose as a way to reduce teacher tenure in Washington, DC?

According to the pro-education reform documentary *Waiting for "Superman,"* one out of every 57 doctors loses his or her license to practice medicine.

One out of every 97 lawyers loses their license to practice law.

In many major cities, only one out of 1000 teachers is fired for performance-related reasons. Why? Tenure.

Tenure Protects Bad Teachers

Tenure is the practice of guaranteeing a teacher their job. Originally, this was a due process guarantee, something intended to work as a check against administrators capriciously firing teachers and replacing them with friends or family members. It was also designed to protect teachers who took political stands the community might disagree with. Tenure as we understand it today was first seen at the university level, where professors would work for years and publish many pieces of inspired academic work before being awarded what amounted to a job for life.

At the elementary and high school levels, tenure has evolved from the original understanding of "due process" to the university-style "job for life." In most states, teachers are awarded tenure after only a few years, at which time they become almost impossible to fire. The main function of these laws is to help bad teachers keep their jobs.

Consider New York City. The *New York Daily News* reports that "over the past three years [2007–2010], just 88 out of some 80,000 city schoolteachers have lost their jobs for poor performance."

Things are no better in New York as a whole. The Albany *Times Union* looked at what was going on outside New York City and discovered some shocking data: Of 132,000 teachers, only 32 were fired for any reason between 2006 and 2011.

Or look at Chicago. In a school district that has by any measure failed its students—only 28.5 percent of 11th graders met or exceeded expectations on that state's standardized tests—*Newsweek* reported that only 0.1 percent of teachers were dismissed for performance-related reasons between 2005 and 2008. When barely one in four students nearing graduation can read and do math, how is it possible that only one in one thousand teachers is worthy of dismissal?

In 2003, one Los Angeles union representative said: "If I'm representing them, it's impossible to get them out. It's impossible. Unless they commit a lewd act." Unfortunately for the students who have to learn from these educators, virtually every teacher who works for the Los Angeles Unified School District receives tenure: In 2009, the *Los Angeles Times* reported that fewer than two percent of teachers are denied tenure during the two-year probationary period after being hired. And once they have tenure, there's no getting rid of them. Between 1995 and 2005, only 112 Los Angeles tenured teachers faced termination—eleven per year—out of 43,000. And that's in a school district where the graduation rate in 2003 was just 51 percent.

One New Jersey union representative was even blunter about the work his organization does to keep bad teachers in the classroom, saying: "I've gone in and defended teachers who shouldn't even be pumping gas."

In ten years, only about 47 out of 100,000 teachers were actually terminated from New Jersey's schools. Original research conducted by the Center for Union Facts (CUF) confirms that almost no one ever gets fired in Newark, New Jersey's largest school district, no matter how bad. Over four recent years, CUF discovered, Newark's school district successfully fired about one out of every 3,000 tenured teachers annually. Graduation statistics indicate that the district needs much stronger medicine: Between the 2001–2002 and the 2004–2005 school years, Newark's graduation rate (not counting the diplomas "earned" through New Jersey's laughable remedial exam) was a mere 30.6 percent.

The evidence that tenure laws keep bad teachers in schools is overwhelming. In New York State, outside of New York City, only about 17 tenured teachers are terminated annually. New York City's chancellor has revealed that in that city, only ten out of 55,000 tenured teachers were terminated in the 2006–2007 school year. In any given year in Florida, scholar Richard Kahlenberg wrote, the involuntary dismissal rate for teachers was an abysmally low 0.05 percent, "compared with 7.9 percent in the Florida workforce as a whole." In Dallas, even when unofficial pressures to resign are factored in, only 0.78 percent of tenured teachers are terminated. Out of Tucson, Arizona's 2,300 tenured teachers, only seven have been fired for classroom behavior in the past five years. Des Moines, Iowa, a school district with almost 3,000 teachers, has fired just two for poor performance in five years.

Teachers Agree: Bad Apples Stay

A study conducted by Public Agenda in 2003 polled 1,345 schoolteachers on a variety of education issues, including the role that tenure played in their schools. When asked, "Does tenure mean that a teacher has worked hard and proved themselves to be very good at what they do?," 58 percent of the teachers polled answered that no, tenure "does not necessarily" mean that. In a related question, 78 percent said a few (or more) teachers in their schools "fail to do a good job and are simply going through the motions."

When Terry Moe, the author of *Special Interest: Teachers Unions and America's Public Schools*, asked teachers what they

Seniority Factor

How seniority is considered in determining which teachers to lay off during a reduction in force, by state.

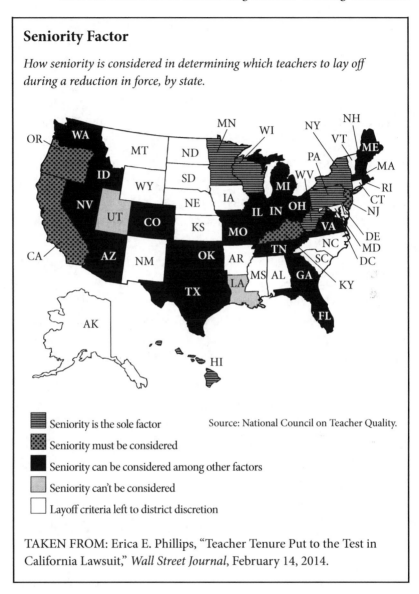

Seniority is the sole factor

Seniority must be considered

Seniority can be considered among other factors

Seniority can't be considered

Layoff criteria left to district discretion

Source: National Council on Teacher Quality.

TAKEN FROM: Erica E. Phillips, "Teacher Tenure Put to the Test in California Lawsuit," *Wall Street Journal*, February 14, 2014.

thought of tenure, they admitted that the Byzantine process of firing bad apples was too time-consuming: 55 percent of teachers, and 47 percent of union members, answered yes when asked, "Do you think tenure and teacher organizations make it too difficult to weed out mediocre and incompetent teachers?"

So why don't districts try to terminate more of their poor performers? The sad answer is that their chance of prevailing is vanishingly small. Teachers' unions have ensured that even with a victory, the process is prohibitively expensive and time-consuming. In the 2006–2007 school year, for example, New York City fired only 10 of its 55,000 tenured teachers. The cost to eliminate those employees averages out to $163,142, according to *Education Week*. According to the Albany *Times Union*, the average process for firing a teacher in New York State outside of New York City proper lasts 502 days and costs more than $216,000. In Illinois, Scott Reeder of the Small Newspaper Group found it costs an average of $219,504 in legal fees alone to get a termination case past all the union-supported hurdles. Columbus, Ohio's own teachers' union president admitted to the Associated Press that firing a tenured teacher can cost as much as $50,000. A spokesman for Idaho school administrators told local press that districts have been known to spend "$100,000 or $200,000" in litigation costs just to get rid of a bad teacher.

It's difficult even to entice the unions to give up tenure for more money. In Washington, D.C., school chancellor Michelle Rhee proposed a voluntary two-tier track for teachers. On one tier, teachers could simply do nothing: maintain regular raises and keep their tenure. On the other track, teachers could give up tenure and be paid according to how well they and their students performed with the potential to earn as much as $140,000 per year. The union wouldn't even let that proposal come up for a vote, however, stubbornly blocking efforts to ratify a new contract for more than three years. When it finally did come up for ratification by the rank and file, the two-tier plan wasn't even an option.

Incompetent Teachers Harm Students

Most teachers absolutely deserve to keep their jobs, and some have begun to speak out about the absurdity of teacher tenure, but it's impossible to pretend that the number of firings actually reflects the number of bad teachers protected by tenure. As long as union leaders possess the legal ability to drag out termination proceedings for months or even years—during which time districts must continue paying teachers, substitute teachers to replace them, and lawyers to arbitrate the proceedings—the situation for students will not improve.

Even Al Shanker, the legendary former president of the American Federation of Teachers, admitted, "a lot of people who have been hired as teachers are basically not competent."

Periodical and Internet Sources Bibliography

The following articles have been selected to supplement the diverse views presented in this chapter.

David Alm	"One Adjunct's Rant, but Not Mine," *Contrary*, February 3, 2013.
Olivia Blanchard	"I Quit Teach For America," *Atlantic*, September 23, 2013.
Susan Edelman and Michael Gartland	"It's Nearly Impossible to Fire Tenured Teachers," *New York Post*, June 14, 2014.
Max Ehrenfreund	"Why Teach For America Is Suddenly Having Trouble Recruiting College Students," *Washington Post*, February 9, 2015.
Peter Greene	"It's Not the Firing; It's the Threatening," *Huffington Post*, August 5, 2014.
Frederick M. Hess and Sarah Dupre	"The Crazy Campus Crusade Against Teach For America," *National Review*, February 11, 2015.
Tyler Kingkade	"9 Reasons Why Being an Adjunct Faculty Member Is Terrible," *Huffington Post*, November 11, 2013.
Joshua Pechthalt and Dean Vogel	"Bizarre Ruling on Tenure: Opposing View," *USA Today*, June 16, 2014.
Justin Peligri	"Underpaid and Overworked: Adjunct Professors Share Their Stories," *USA Today*, July 17, 2014.
Gary Rhoades	"Adjunct Professors Are the New Working Poor," CNN, September 25, 2013.
Elizabeth Segran	"The Adjunct Revolt: How Poor Professors Are Fighting Back," *Atlantic*, April 28, 2014.

CHAPTER 3

What Are Ethical Issues Surrounding Testing?

Chapter Preface

The General Educational Development (GED) tests are four tests that certify that the test taker has the equivalent of the academic skills he or she would possess upon graduation from high school. The tests serve as a way to certify the skills of individuals who have not graduated from high school, and passing the test is a requirement for many jobs.

In 2014 the GED Testing Service launched a new test, which is more expensive and completely computerized. The test is also significantly more challenging for test takers.

Some commenters have argued that the changes in the test are a good thing. James E. Causey, writing for the *Milwaukee Journal Sentinel*, remarks that "the test has to get tougher because it needs to reflect the changes that have occurred in the job market." He adds, "Employers are demanding more out of their workers than they did 10 years ago or even two years ago. The changes also may make a young person think twice about dropping out of school on the assumption that he or she can 'just get a GED.'" For Causey, then, the more difficult GED test will encourage people to finish high school and will ensure that those who do not finish are actually prepared for the job market.

Others, though, have been critical of the new test. A number of states objected to the increased cost and the lack of a paper-and-pencil option that they feared would prevent many from taking the test. Nine states (New York, New Hampshire, Missouri, Iowa, Montana, Indiana, Louisiana, Maine, and West Virginia) dropped the test altogether and decided instead to use tests from new companies that now compete with the GED Testing Service.

Another argument is that the new GED does not address the real problems associated with the old test. University of Chicago economist James J. Heckman and his colleagues wrote an essay that questioned whether the GED really showed preparation for the work world. Heckman and his coauthors argued that the GED measures scholarly abilities, but that "the GED test—and achievement tests in general—miss skills like motivation, persistence, self-esteem, time management and self-control. A growing body of evidence has shown that these types of skills can be measured and that they rival raw intelligence in determining success in the labor market and school." Heckman and his colleagues said that high school dropouts need intervention and help with life skills that the GED cannot capture or foster.

The following chapter examines other ethical issues involving standardized tests, including whether they assure or interfere with student learning and whether teachers should be judged or evaluated based on student test performance.

"[Chicago Public Schools] teachers have reported being forced into teaching their students testing strategies, at the expense of teaching content and processes to enable students to meet standards."

Teachers Take an Ethical Stand Against Testing

Chicago Teachers Union

Chicago Teachers Union (CTU) is the labor union representing teachers and other workers in the Chicago public school system. In the following viewpoint, CTU argues that testing does not measure real learning. CTU further maintains that testing takes up instructional time and actually decreases teachers' abilities to focus on meaningful instruction. CTU contends that testing is a distraction from issues such as income inequality, poverty, and poor health that actually hold some students back.

As you read, consider the following questions:

1. Before the accountability era, what were the educational reforms with the most momentum, according to CTU?

"CTU Position Paper: Debunking the Myths of Standardized Testing," Ctunet.com. Copyright © Chicago Teachers Union. Reproduced by permission.

2. In CTU's view, what factors beyond teachers' control influence student achievement?

3. What does CTU say is the important lesson to derive from testing scandals?

Picture the school you would like all children to attend. Do you envision a place where curiosity is piqued, creativity is developed, problems are debated and solved and multiple perspectives are respected? What about daily drilling for standardized tests, exposure only to subjects that are tested (that leaves out social studies, art, music, library, and physical education), reading passages instead of books, and math and science procedures but not unifying concepts?

The Rise of Testing

In the last twenty years, the U.S. has made a dramatic shift toward a reliance on standardized test scores as a measure of teaching effectiveness and school improvement. The "accountability movement" began in the 1970s but spread rapidly in the 1990s and became consolidated into law by No Child Left Behind in 2002. Led not by educators but by the business sector, the major players in education "reform" legislation were members of the Business Coalition for Education Reform, the Business Roundtable, the U.S. Chamber of Commerce, and many state chambers of commerce.

Prior to the accountability era, the educational reforms with the most momentum were influenced by the civil rights movement. Desegregation, affirmative action, and programs like Head Start challenged the inequities of American society. Scores on the National Assessment of Educational Progress (NAEP) show that the achievement gap shrank through the 1970s and 1980s. Teenaged black students through the late 1970s and 1980s, the first cohort to accrue the benefits of the social reforms of the civil rights era, experienced the most significant growth during that time.

The era of accountability through the last two federal education policies, No Child Left Behind (NCLB) and now Race to the Top, has greatly inflated standardized test-taking and "test-prep" curricula without evidence connecting it to real learning. Standardized testing grew out of the American tradition of using quantitative attempts to measure 'intelligence' as a pretext for racist and exclusionary policies. Today's tests still discriminate, and together with inequities in housing, employment, education, and health care, contribute to the "achievement gap." Overreliance on standardized tests has led to reduced graduation rates among students of color, narrowed the curriculum in all subjects and grade levels and ill prepared our students for fulfilling careers and civic engagement. The reforms of the accountability era are harmful policies that lead to neither short-term successes nor long-term prosperity for students.

Politicians have become increasingly "outraged" at the number of low-income children and students of color who are not academically prepared to attend college. Instead of looking at some of the many serious issues these students face on a daily basis, or looking to decrease societal inequities or instituting research-based strategies for school improvement (such as smaller classes), the corporate-led "reform" movement is blaming the teachers. This "business model" approach to education is data obsessed and purports that the solution to inequities in education is to fire teachers whose students have low test scores and reward teachers whose students have high test scores. They continue to promote top-down approaches to quick fixes, ignoring decades of research. The way to achieve sustainable improvement is through long-term processes such as developing teaching quality, empowering community and families, mandating smaller class sizes, improving resource access for schools and communities in need, and implementing a joyous, critical, inquiry-based and creative learning experience for students.

High-Stakes Testing and the Achievement Gap

Corporate reform groups such as Advance Illinois and Stand for Children claim teachers are the main factor in student academic achievement. Recent research shows otherwise: As much as 90% of variation in student growth is explained by factors outside the control of teachers. Children who do not have access to health care, who are hungry, who are exhausted from nighttime symptoms of asthma, who are fearful of violence in their communities, who do not have books or access to other informal learning at home, whose parents have limited education, whose families are constantly stressed by economic problems, and who do not go to libraries and museums in their free time are at an academic disadvantage.

These factors are highly related not only to testing outcomes, academic achievement, future education and socioeconomic success but also to the racial, ethnic and class origins of individuals. The inequitable history of American society, politics, institutions and economic relations are at the root of these relations. As a result, when academic outcomes are averaged across subgroups such as race and class, glaring gaps appear.

Corporate reformers use the academic achievement gap to justify increasing the frequency and consequences of high-stakes testing. These policies have nothing to do with addressing the root causes of how such gaps arise and persist in society, nor do they improve student learning. In fact these policies typically worsen academic outcomes for students impacted by them.

According to the National Center for Fair and Open Testing, black and Latino students, especially those from low-income families, have suffered enormously from the nation's increase in high-stakes testing and the inordinate amount of time spent on test prep. The tests have resulted in an increase in dropout rates for these populations, an increase in expulsion and "counseling out" of schools seeking to increase their test scores, an increase in grade retention, cheating by principals, an increase in special education placement, limited course content and a decrease in access to merit-based scholarships and thus a bigger economic barrier to attending college. It has also been shown that earning a low performance label attached to low standardized test results can discourage urban low-income students from enrolling in college.

High-Stakes Tests Cannot Adequately Measure Knowledge

Test scores fail as measures of learning when high-stakes testing dominates curricula and instructional practice. When practices driven by testing are widespread, test score gains do not represent a corresponding growth in the broader domain of knowledge that tests are supposed to sample and measure. With extensive use of coaching, test scores may not even reflect true gains in the narrow subject matter of the particular test.

In a comprehensive survey, CPS [Chicago Public Schools] teachers were found to have devoted large amounts of time to prepping students for the ACT [a college readiness assessment test]; typically, over a month of instructional time was devoted to test prep. The outcome? More test prep was associated with lower ACT scores.

Research shows students who are tasked with intellectually demanding work that promotes disciplined inquiry and relevance to their lives score higher on standardized tests. CPS teachers have reported being forced into teaching their students testing strategies, at the expense of teaching content and processes to enable students to meet standards.

"Strategies like skimming for information, eliminating irrelevant answers, reading answers first then checking for content in the question. Students are not taught to think critically or deeply at this time. They are presented with so much information over

a broad range of topics that is loaded into their short-term memory to be forgotten as soon as the standardized test is completed," reported a CPS teacher of middle school environmental science, biology and pre-engineering.

The frequency of standardized testing, and the instructional time devoted to test prep, crowds out the use of authentic formative assessments that help teachers carefully advance student learning.

Constant high-stakes testing causes students to interpret all their assessments as summative rather than as interactions meant to help their learning process, eroding the value of formative assessments to the teacher and student.

Testing Scandals

Schools and districts across the country have been caught cheating (changing test answers or giving their students test problems ahead of time), including in Atlanta, Philadelphia, Washington, D.C., and Texas. A March 2011 *USA Today* investigation proved that the dramatic rise in Washington, D.C., test scores was due to cheating, not to Michelle Rhee's "no excuses" administration. Statisticians have said that the probability that the number of erasures on tests from specific schools and specific grades could be due to anything but cheating is as likely as winning the lottery's Powerball. There have also been instances where tests were scored incorrectly, failing and sending students who had actually passed the tests to summer school.

In October 2010, the *Chicago Tribune* reported that when Illinois adjusted the ISAT [Illinois Standards Achievement Test] scoring system in 2006, it "lowered the number of points required to pass" resulting in more students appearing as if they were "proficient" than before. A recent study by the [University of] Chicago Consortium on School Research found that, after correcting for the differences in assessments and

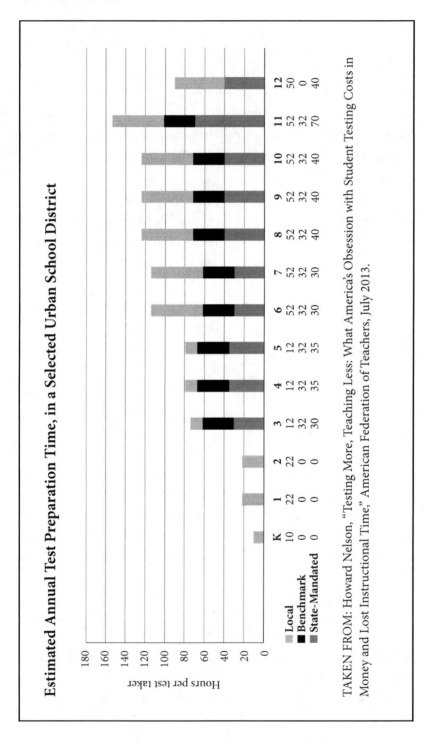

Estimated Annual Test Preparation Time, in a Selected Urban School District

	K	1	2	3	4	5	6	7	8	9	10	11	12
Local	10	22	22	12	12	12	52	52	52	52	52	52	50
Benchmark	0	0	0	32	32	32	32	32	32	32	32	32	0
State-Mandated	0	0	0	30	35	35	30	30	40	40	40	70	40

Hours per test taker

TAKEN FROM: Howard Nelson, "Testing More, Teaching Less: What America's Obsession with Student Testing Costs in Money and Lost Instructional Time," American Federation of Teachers, July 2013.

changing demographics, there was essentially no increase in scores of elementary students over two decades of test-driven reform.

Some tests, such as in Mississippi, have such low thresholds for scoring high that despite ranking high on the percentage of students meeting state standards, they were at the bottom based on the NAEP test results. There were 35 states that set the proficiency level on state tests in 2009 way below what would be considered 'basic' on the NAEP equivalent score.

Even without high-profile scandals such as those mentioned [previously], the use of test scores for accountability threatens the validity of test results. Daniel Koretz, a scholar in educational measurement, has been testifying about the effect of high-stakes testing on narrowing instruction and its harm to student learning for over two decades. Highly regarded national institutions and associations, such as the National Board on Educational Testing and Public Policy, the National Academy of Sciences, the American Educational Research Association, the Economic Policy Institute, the Association for Childhood Education International, and the Education Sector have been writing for decades about the pitfalls of both standardized testing in general and the overreliance on standardized testing, especially in using these tests to make major high-stakes decisions such as high school graduation or teacher evaluation.

The policy makers have not listened. Even though the media reports on testing scandals, the editorial boards of the nation's newspapers still support a system of "increased accountability," which they equate with test scores. This type of response is not new. When score inflation became apparent in the early '90s in response to what was relatively low-stakes accountability, the policy makers refused to acknowledge the problem.

The important lesson about these scandals is that standardized testing and accountability policies make test results useless for making valid inferences about real student learning and hurt students.

Deliberately Low Expectations

Why do corporate interests continue to push toward a test-centered public education system that is clearly harmful to students? The reality of their agenda is to align the outputs of public education with the needs of an unequal and highly polarized economic system. The soaring income inequality in recent decades that continues to benefit the upper class has been driven primarily by job polarization. There has been rapid growth in low-skilled low-wage work while middle-wage jobs are disappearing under global competition. Even jobs requiring postsecondary education are driven down into low-wage work. Within such an economic system, for the people who control the majority of wealth and the direction of public policy, large investment in educating the majority of working-class children does not make economic sense. As educator Lois Weiner has succinctly put it, global-scale Walmart jobs require no more than an 8th grade education. The missteps of corporate education reformers are not due to their oversight of evidence but are simply cold calculation. If the standards and livelihoods they envision for our children are limited to "McJobs," it seems they do not need the kinds of interdisciplinary, authentic project-based learning and critical inquiry that are prevalent in the prestigious schools the privileged send their children to. Teachers and parents have much higher expectations and demands for the public education of all children.

| "*Instead of cultivating fear by spreading misinformation and arguing for less and less accountability, union leaders and their supporters should honor their commitments to our children and parents.*"

Teachers Unions Sacrifice High Standards to Evade Accountability

Hanna Skandera and Kevin Huffman

Hanna Skandera heads the New Mexico Department of Public Education. Kevin Huffman is a lawyer who served as commissioner of the Tennessee Department of Education until 2015. In the following viewpoint, they argue that teachers who oppose testing are standing in the way of student progress. They argue that the Common Core State Standards Initiative and testing to make sure students reach the standards are part of a program to improve learning and student outcomes. They conclude that testing is in the best interest of students and that teachers' unions are in the way of progress.

Hanna Skandera and Kevin Huffman, "Teachers Unions Sacrifice High Standards to Evade Accountability," *Washington Post*, July 24, 2014. Washingtonpost.com. Copyright © 2014 The Washington Post. Reproduced by permission.

As you read, consider the following questions:

1. What do the authors say was the big news coming out of the National Education Association convention?

2. What do the authors say New Mexico unions are doing to oppose testing and standards?

3. What positive results do the authors point to in Tennessee and New Mexico as evidence of the value of standards and testing?

You can always count on the national teachers' unions to behave badly at their annual conventions, and they certainly didn't let us down this month. In doing so, however, they let down many of their members, along with students who are working hard to meet higher expectations.

In classrooms across the United States, higher academic standards are inspiring students and teachers. Students are more engaged and excited in school, raising their hands more often, asking more questions, thinking critically and solving problems instead of just memorizing facts. Teachers feel more motivated, creative and empowered to develop new and better ways to reach their students.

This progress is at risk, however, because of a destructive change of heart by union leaders who are prepared to sacrifice high standards for students so that adults can evade accountability.

Under pressure from the militant wing of her union, American Federation of Teachers president Randi Weingarten took the cynical step this month of backing away from support for the Common Core State Standards, announcing a new fund for teachers to critique and rewrite the standards. This is the latest and most visible step in a year-long campaign by the union to discredit the implementation of higher academic standards and—most important—the measurement of student progress against these higher standards.

Meanwhile, the big news coming out of the National Education Association convention one week earlier was a resolution calling for the resignation of education secretary Arne Duncan. The union's bosses have been cross with Duncan before, but most recently, he issued mildly supportive comments on a legal decision that threw out California's teacher tenure and seniority laws because of their appalling impact on poor and minority students.

The NEA also voted in Lily Eskelsen García as its new national president. In her first day on the job, Eskelsen García referred to value-added measures, a common measure of teacher effectiveness, as "the mark of the devil."

Unfortunately, this sort of over-the-top rhetoric is eminently predictable. Union leaders' enthusiasm for reforms often wanes as we move from the planning (and spending) phase into measuring student progress.

In Tennessee, as part of a successful Race to the Top grant, union leaders signed on to high standards and evaluation, and the state developed a nationally recognized training plan for teachers led by exceptional educators. But this past school year, union leaders called for a delay in administering better assessments. The union also sued the state to block the evaluation system it previously supported. As a result, Tennessee children will continue to take easier fill-in-the-bubble tests while taxpayer dollars are spent on lawyers.

In New Mexico, a nationally recognized transition plan was created with the help of talented educators. A local union leader also worked with the state's largest district to implement the plan; another co-authored (with one of us) an op-ed touting the measures of New Mexico's current teacher evaluation system as a "common-sense answer."

Today, however, the unions in New Mexico are staging town halls to stir up parents with misinformation about higher standards and testing, even though the overall amount of testing has decreased since the new standards were adopted.

Race to the Top

The ARRA [American Recovery and Reinvestment Act of 2009] provides $4.35 billion for the Race to the Top Fund, a competitive grant program designed to encourage and reward states that are creating the conditions for education innovation and reform; achieving significant improvement in student outcomes, including making substantial gains in student achievement, closing achievement gaps, improving high school graduation rates, and ensuring student preparation for success in college and careers; and implementing ambitious plans in four core education reform areas:

- adopting standards and assessments that prepare students to succeed in college and the workplace and to compete in the global economy;
- building data systems that measure student growth and success, and inform teachers and principals about how they can improve instruction;
- recruiting, developing, rewarding, and retaining effective teachers and principals, especially where they are needed most; and
- turning around our lowest-achieving schools.

Race to the Top will reward states that have demonstrated success in raising student achievement and have the best plans to accelerate their reforms in the future. These states will offer models for others to follow and will spread the best reform ideas across their states and across the country.

US Department of Education,
Race to the Top Program Executive Summary,
November 2009.

Clearer standards and better assessments offer students, parents and teachers exactly what they want: less testing and less test prep.

Astonishingly, the unions seem to think that they can ask for more taxpayer money while simultaneously weakening measurement and accountability. This is the very course of action that has led the United States to its middling level of performance on international benchmarks.

In our states, this backtracking also comes despite significant student gains. Tennessee had the most growth of any state in the country on last year's National Assessment of Educational Progress. New Mexico high school juniors achieved record gains on state tests, and graduation rates rose dramatically after the standards were raised on New Mexico's state exam.

Instead of cultivating fear by spreading misinformation and arguing for less and less accountability, union leaders and their supporters should honor their commitments to our children and parents. They should honor their commitments to employers who rely on our education system to prepare young people to compete in the global economy. They should honor their commitments to civil rights leaders and advocates for the disabled who have fought for decades for greater equity in education, and to parents, who have the right to know how their children are performing.

U.S. teachers and students are ready. They are proving it every day. It's time to stop attacking higher standards and accountability and focus on helping our children reach their potential.

> "Without guidance and information, parents are unable to sort through fact and fiction, rumors and politics. Sadly, this confusion might unravel a potentially good program."

Opposition to Testing Is Well Intentioned but Unorganized

Laura McKenna

Laura McKenna is a writer and a former political science professor. In the following viewpoint, she says that there is a good deal of opposition to the Common Core State Standards Initiative. This opposition, she says, is mostly uninformed and confused. She rejects the idea that standardized testing takes up too much instructional time and says that parents are being influenced by teachers, who dislike the idea that test performance may be tied to teacher pay. She concludes that the government needs to do better in communicating with parents about the Common Core standards.

Laura McKenna, © 2015 The Atlantic Media Co., as first published in The Atlantic Magazine. All rights reserved. Distributed by Tribune Content Agency, LLC. Reproduced by permission.

As you read, consider the following questions:

1. According to the viewpoint, what does Arne Duncan believe is the reason suburban moms distrust the Common Core?

2. Why does McKenna say new testing will not much change the American school experience?

3. What does McKenna identify as a major flaw in the implementation of the Common Core standards?

This March [2015], millions of schoolkids will take new standardized tests that are designed to accompany the Common Core [State] Standards [Initiative]. As that deadline looms, anxiety grows in suburban communities. Conspiracy theories, too, have grown out of parents' natural instinct to protect their children from bureaucracies and self-styled experts. A teacher backlash against the school reform efforts and the lack of leadership on this issue have made it more difficult for parents to get facts.

Common Core

The Common Core standards are, of course, a set of broad, universal academic goals in math and English language arts for public school students of all ages. With the standards come national standardized tests that, in theory, will allow policy makers to compare performance across states and different demographics. Forty-three states, as well as the District of Columbia, have signed onto the Common Core program, and most of them have joined one of two testing "consortiums" known by their (rather unfortunate) acronyms: the PARCC [Partnership for Assessment of Readiness for College and Careers] or the SBAC [Smarter Balanced Assessment Consortium]. But the process has been far from smooth. More than half of the 26 states that initially signed onto the PARCC exam in 2010 have dropped out; only a dozen states will use the test this spring. Seventeen other states will take the SBAC, which has also sparked controversy, while the remaining ones will use their own tests.

Among the most vocal opponents to the new standards are conservative, Tea Party Republicans, who are ideologically opposed to any expansion of the federal government—something they inaccurately equate to the Common Core initiative. And these politically motivated critics, who have rallied against a national system of learning standards for decades, have their own conspiracy theories about the Common Core, too. These include claims that the standards will turn students gay, that it preaches an anti-American agenda, and that Muslim Brotherhood and Communists shaped the content. Complicating matters, other state-level politicians have fought against a uniform system of standards and tests because they're wary of seeing how the kids in their turf stack up against children elsewhere. No Child Left Behind did little to unify learning systems across the states, and what remains are essentially 50 different sets of standards and 50 different systems for measuring achievement. That makes it all but impossible to compare test results in, say, Connecticut and Texas. And with the huge variations in how much states spend on education, it seems illogical to assume that kids across the nation, regardless of where they reside, will perform equally well on a test such as the PARCC.

Suburban Parents Against Standards

Now, amid all the backlash, an unlikely subculture appears to be emerging in the anti–Common Core world: suburban parents. Even U.S. education secretary Arne Duncan has taken note of the trend, who last November told a group of superintendents that "white suburban moms" were resisting the implementation of the Common Core. His theory? "All of a sudden ... their child isn't as brilliant as they thought they were, and their school isn't quite as good as they thought they were."

Tea Party conservatives and suburban parents might not have a lot in common, but they seem to increasingly share a distrust of bureaucracy. I happen to live in a middle-class suburb outside of New York City—one that could easily be considered the capital of "white suburban moms." And I'm realizing Duncan was on to something: Their wrath is real, and it's based largely on misperception and widespread fearmongering perpetuated by the Tea Party skeptics and anxious state policy makers.

My friends and neighbors post links almost daily on Facebook to articles claiming the Common Core "curriculum," as they perceive it, is destroying American youth. It has single-handedly taken recess away from kids, they argue. The upcoming tests demoralize kids and teachers. The new curricula and tests are an assault on an otherwise idyllic world where kids used to learn naturally—like those lucky children in Finland. Instead of actually instilling knowledge in students, teachers drill irrelevant facts into kids' heads in order to game the testing results. And since the new exams will be taken on computers, hackers might even reveal the test results to colleges. While there may be elements of truth in some of those parents' fears, these protests have developed an irrational, hysterical bent. And they often have very real implications when it comes to public policy; these theories and fears have already led to political action at the local level. Parents have formed groups that claim to disseminate "the facts" about the Common Core. They share tips for opting out of the tests. They read prepared speeches at school board meetings. One local debate on the Common Core hosted by the League of Women Voters was standing room only.

The reality of the Common Core model is much more boring. America's schools could be better, no doubt. They could be more equal. They could be more effective in preparing kids for the new, global economy and the ever growing rigors of higher education. But there is no evidence that one set of standards, that a single standardized test, will alter the basic school experience of children. They will probably still have to do book reports on Abraham Lincoln and *To Kill a Mockingbird*. They almost certainly will still have time to joke around on the playground with their buddies. They will be evaluated by teachers' exams and rubrics and probably won't be penalized by the Common Core tests.

Testing Is Common Already

One common fear I've heard among parents is that the Common Core represents a new emphasis on standardized testing that takes away from learning time. But, in America, kids of all ages already take standardized tests; schools have long administered state assessments. And that's on top of the alphabet soup of nationally accepted proficiency exams: the SATs, ACTs, GREs, GMATs, LSATs, you name it. The new Common Core tests do not threaten to significantly alter the American school experience. The PARCC test for its part doesn't require much more time than previous assessments. In the past, all public school students in New Jersey, for example, took a state-designed standardized math and reading test. Fifth-grade students had 316 minutes to fill in the bubbles on an answer sheet. The PARCC's fifth-grade test, meanwhile, will take 405 minutes. That might seem like a big difference for a 10-year-old, but the 89-minute difference doesn't have much impact on the 180-day school year. That's about a quarter of the time that my teenage boys like to spend playing *Super Mario Bros.* on any given Saturday.

So, why are suburban parents suddenly taken with test anxiety? Duncan reasoned that "white suburban moms"—and, presumably, dads as well—fear their children will perform poorly on the Common Core tests. But based on my conversations with parents and school administrators, as well as my observations of local school board meetings, I believe parental fears are broader and more complex than Duncan made them out to be.

" MY FATHER SAYS, THESE INTELLIGENCE
TESTS ARE BIASED TOWARD THE INTELLIGENT. "

© Edgar Argo, "My father says, these intelligence tests are biased toward the intelligent,"
CartoonStock.com.

A typical suburban parent, like all parents, has an intense, natural instinct to protect his or her kids. We parents are hardwired to protect our babies from the unknown—and for the most part, this is a good thing. After all, protection of offspring and suspicion of outsiders have kept the human species alive for millions of years. But this instinct sometimes takes parents in the wrong direction. Just look at the anti-vaccination movement: Though the instincts of anti-vaccination parent activists are pure, their actions have resulted in what's arguably a public health crisis in the country.

Many parents view the Common Core and the accompanying tests as a threat to their ability to keep their kids safe in a hostile world. Suburban parents, who are known for being particularly involved in their kids' education and traditionally enjoy a good deal of influence on district policy making, are frustrated by not being able to convince their local school boards to alter the standards or testing requirements. They worry that they won't be able to help kids with homework, because the new learning materials rely on teaching methods foreign to them. They worry that, ultimately, their kids will be unemployed and living in the basement in their 20s.

Then social media steps in. There are those Facebook posts promoting articles with click-bait titles like "Parents Opting Kids Out of Common Core Face Threats from Schools" or "Common Core Tests Fail Kids in New York Again. Here's How" or "5 Reasons the Common Core Is Ruining Childhood." I can picture it in my head: articles with stock photos of children sitting miserably at a desk or ominous images of broken pencils. These articles go viral in certain communities—not least in suburbia, where parents like (and have the time) to stay on top of things and are often used to getting their way. Virtual networking makes it all too easy to be outraged these days.

Tea Party conservatives and suburban parents might not have a lot in common, but they seem to increasingly share a distrust of bureaucracy, so-called experts, and federal rules. The sources of their opposition, of course, are entirely different: For Tea Party conservatives, it's about ideology; for parents, it's about protection. Politics makes for strange bedfellows, indeed. Teachers have fostered parental protests, too. Teachers' unions were initially very supportive of the Common Core, and educators helped shape its goals. However, support from educators began to wane in the past year, when state legislatures started to create policies tying test scores to their pay, largely through new teacher evaluation systems. The new stipulations have caused unrest among teachers across the country, including those in my suburban New Jersey school district, adding a new layer of politics to the Common Core.

Teacher Disapproval

A recent nationwide poll conducted by researchers at *Education Next* found that teachers' approval rate of the Common Core dropped from 76 percent in 2013 to only 46 percent in 2014. Paul Peterson, one of the *Education Next* researchers and the director of Harvard's Program on Education Policy and Governance in the Graduate School of Education, confirmed that teachers are dissatisfied with the evaluation component. But, Peterson added, they're also more informed than the general public is about the standards and accompanying tests.

Parents take their cues about education from their children's teachers, and unfortunately that often means important facts are lost in translation once they exit the classroom. The bottom line is that if the teachers aren't happy, the parents aren't happy either.

Ultimately, the blurring between Common Core fact and fiction reveals a major flaw in the implementation of the program. No one group or individual took the lead in informing parents what the standards actually look like in the classroom and how it would affect their kids. Without political and education leaders providing valid, fact-based justifications for the new testing system and a clear, jargon-free explanation of new teaching strategies, suburban parents are easily influenced by others.

Parents need to understand why a new universal set of standards is important, particularly parents in good school districts where schools are working well. They need to know how their kids will benefit from this program—and if their kids won't benefit, parents need to know why these test results serve the larger public good, that they can help shape policies that will help others. Parents need to know that their kids will continue to be graded based on their teachers' assessments and that the tests really serve to provide data for administrators and political leaders who can set policies based on students' overall performance. Parents need to know how the Common Core differs from previous state curricula and how it will affect their kids on a daily basis. Simple facts—that the Common Core does not prescribe certain textbooks, for example—would go a long way in dispelling confusion.

Perhaps the "white suburban mom" protests will dissipate after the test results are publicized. Suburban schools tend to be relatively high achieving and have historically done very well on state-level standardized tests, so there is no reason to believe that the new tests will produce drastically different results. Parents in these areas, moreover, often supplement their children's education with tutors and other resources. These schools will do fine on any national comparison.

But without guidance and information, parents are unable to sort through fact and fiction, rumors and politics. Sadly, this confusion might unravel a potentially good program.

| *"In his mind, loyalty to his students justified cheating."*

Teachers Cheat on Tests as a Reaction to Poor Education Policy

Robert Prentice

Robert Prentice is a professor and department chair in the Mc-Combs School of Business, University of Texas at Austin. In the following viewpoint, he discusses the scandal in Atlanta, where teachers cheated to improve student test scores. He says that by putting so much emphasis on student test scores, teachers were incentivized to cheat in order to prevent students from being labeled failures and to keep schools from being closed. This is especially the case since studies show teachers can have only a small effect on test scores at best. Teachers felt they needed to cheat to protect their students from arbitrary and unfair consequences. Prentice concludes that cheating is wrong, but the government's testing initiative is also misguided and arguably immoral.

As you read, consider the following questions:

1. Why are the worst schools bad, according to Prentice?

Robert Prentice, "Why Good Teachers Do Bad Things," *Ethics Unwrapped*, August 19, 2014. Ethicsunwrapped.utexas.edu. Copyright © 2014 The University of Texas at Austin–McCombs School of Business. Reproduced by permission.

2. According to Prentice, what rationalization for cheating did Damany Lewis use?

3. How did incrementalism play a role in the cheating scandal, in Prentice's view?

Rachel Aviv's article "Wrong Answer" in a recent *New Yorker* issue [July 21, 2014] presents a textbook case of why good people do bad things. The article tells the story of the recent cheating scandal in the Atlanta School District, which was one of the worst of a string of school cheating scandals across the U.S. Forty-four of the district's schools cheated. One hundred and ten teachers were put on administrative leave. Many were fired. Thirty-three teachers and administrators were charged criminally, including the district's superintendent, Beverly Hall. More than half of the defendants pled guilty; others still await trial.

Not Bad People

The scandal did not happen because a bunch of people with particularly bad character were teaching in the Atlanta schools. The teachers and administrators featured in the article appear to have been committed to education and to helping students.

The scandal did not happen because people were unable to decide whether cheating (by giving their students access to standardized tests before they took them and changing answers after they took them) was right or wrong. Everyone knows cheating is wrong.

The story is one of behavioral ethics and it begins with incentives. As Lamar Pierce notes in our [*Ethics Unwrapped's*] *Incentive Gaming* video, people respond to incentives. They will often game the system. Anyone setting up a system of incentives needs to think long and hard about how their targets will respond. As I indicate in a four-part video that we will post on this site in September about how to be your best self, effective incentives use measurable metrics and are moderate in scale. If too much is at stake, the temptation to cheat will be large.

From this perspective, the fault largely lies with Congress. The No Child Left Behind law, as implemented around the country, is misguided. Our worst schools are bad because the children who go to them are poor, which saddles them with a range of disadvantages. Rather than improving the schools by attacking poverty, Congress decided to put all the responsibility on teachers, who, according to a document by the American Statistical Association quoted by Aviv, account for only somewhere between one and fourteen percent of variability in standardized test scores. It's not that teachers cannot have any impact, but it is unrealistic to expect them, just by dint of greater effort and motivation, to create the sort of improvement in student test scores that is routinely demanded.

If target scores are not met in Georgia and elsewhere, students are humiliated, schools are shuttered, principals are fired, and teachers' evaluations plummet. This incentive system causes teachers to "teach the test," which has its own set of moral implications. Additionally, it should surprise no one who has studied incentive systems that an unrealistic emphasis on standardized test scores has also been followed by major cheating scandals in Baltimore, Cincinnati, El Paso, Houston, Philadelphia, St. Louis, and Toledo. Cheating has been detected in 40 states and probably went undetected in the other ten.

Rationalizations

But blame lies with the teachers and administrators who cheated as well. Many teachers did not cheat and even tried to turn in the wrongdoers. But Aviv's story of several of those who did cheat makes a case that their main motive was not to keep their own jobs or to get raises, although those motives certainly had to affect their decision making. Rather, their pri-

The Atlanta Cheating Scandal

This leads us to the public school district of Atlanta in the summer of 2011, when the Georgia governor released a report that described widespread cheating on the 2008–2009 state assessment exams—cheating *by teachers*, not students. The extent of the cheating and some of the specific ways in which the cheating took place were reported with an almost gleeful indignation by news agencies around the country. Of the 178 educators implicated in the scandal, most were teachers and 38 were principals; 82 teachers confessed specifically to modifying the exams of their students by erasing and changing answers after the exams had been completed. One school held "erasure parties," complete with pizza, where teachers worked together to "improve" the performances of their students on the exams. And, as one newspaper account reported, the cheating activities moved beyond simply erasing and changing answers: "teachers admitted to placing lower-performing students next to high achievers so they could cheat more easily, pointing to correct answers while students were taking tests, and reading aloud answers during testing." The scandal reached right to the top of the Atlanta school system, leading to the public disgracing of the superintendent, who was cited for turning a blind eye to the cheating.

James M. Lang, Cheating Lessons.
Cambridge, MA: Harvard University Press, 2015.

mary motive to help the kids they taught led to rationalizing of the sort that is common in white-collar crimes. In our videos *Jack and Rationalizations* and the fourth video in the *Being Your Best Self* group (available next month), we talk about the sorts of rationalizations that people commonly use to give themselves permission to do that which they know is wrong, like cheating. Damany Lewis, a math teacher at Parks Middle School in Atlanta, is in many ways the most sympathetic actor in the Atlanta scandal. Smart, hardworking, and fanatically devoted to his students, he used a common "higher loyalty" rationalization. He knew that cheating was wrong, but his students had worked so hard that he felt he had to cheat to prevent them from being crushed by being labeled as "failures," from seeing their neighborhood damaged by the closing of its school, and from being transferred around Atlanta to other schools. In his mind, loyalty to his students justified cheating.

There are many other behavioral ethics lessons in this story. *Obedience to authority* played a role—Lewis's principal supported the cheating and made it clear that teachers who didn't play along could be punished. So did the *conformity bias*—so many schools in Atlanta were cheating that it was easy to view the practice as acceptable. *Incrementalism* played a part—the cheating started modestly, but grew and grew. Finally, there was *loss aversion*—once the teachers and the administrators began receiving plaudits on a national level for making such progress in Atlanta, it became seemingly impossible for them to give up that glory by admitting that the students' progress was mostly an illusion.

These behavioral factors are an explanation for why teachers cheated in Atlanta. They are not an excuse. Cheating is wrong. So is government's refusal to fix the real problems with our schools.

| "We should tie student achievement to bonus pay, not teacher salaries. This is an important distinction."

Tying Teacher Bonus Pay to Test Scores Can Be Done Fairly

Matt Amaral

Matt Amaral is a writer and high school English teacher in the San Francisco Bay area. In the following viewpoint, he argues that tying teacher salaries to performance is a bad idea. He says that tests do not adequately assess student abilities. However, he admits that bonuses for teachers whose students' scores improve might be a good way to reward good teachers, even if assessments are not perfect. Tying teacher salaries to test scores, though, he says, would be unfair and counterproductive as long as assessments are so imperfect.

As you read, consider the following questions:

1. In Amaral's view, why do multiple-choice tests fail to adequately assess his students?

Matt Amaral, "Connecting Test Scores to Teacher Pay—Do It Right, or Not at All," New America Media, May 11, 2011. Newamericamedia.org. Copyright © 2011 New America Media. Reproduced by permission.

2. Why doesn't the incentive of better pay improve teaching, according to Amaral?

3. How does California's Lucia Mar Unified School District tie teacher pay to student performance?

A recent Public Policy Institute of California survey on education shows 69 percent of Californians believe student achievement should be closely tied with teachers' salaries. The finding shows a greater public concern about teacher quality, likely brought on by recent attacks on teachers' unions. This avenue of discourse often blames teachers more than it praises, and it disregards the tough job teachers face in real classrooms.

Tests Do Not Tell Much About Students

I am a teacher in a low-income urban high school. Although I agree student achievement should be partially tied to teachers' salaries, it needs to be one of many measures we use to reward good classroom instruction.

Despite efforts by various foundations and organizations, there still isn't a proven way to effectively evaluate teachers. I wouldn't mind making some extra money when my students' scores rise—why would I? But we have to remember our assessments of both students and teachers are far from perfect.

I give my students many tests. The unfortunate thing about our state and district-wide assessments is they are all multiple choice. In addition, there are often errors in the tests, or the test data is inconclusive.

Some of the tests are culturally biased as well. These tests are so flawed it is sometimes impossible to judge anything from the data gathered. I just did an assessment of data over a whole year for one of my classes, and it didn't show me much. The most one could discern is that students got a little bit better at taking a certain kind of test.

Part of the problem for me and other English teachers is how we assess language arts skills in a multiple-choice test. The actual writing part is either very small or nonexistent. So even though I guided my students in writing seven persuasive essays, each through three drafts, with the series turned in as a portfolio, the students weren't asked to write anything on the statewide test.

To me, testing students on their knowledge of English without requiring any writing is unacceptable. And it is unacceptable for anyone to tell me I am not doing my job, if they haven't seen my students' writing.

Also, the sheer variety of classes we teach make what we do very difficult to assess with the current tests.

For example, in my English department we have three levels of English language learner classes; three levels of sheltered classes for limited-English-proficiency students; regular English; plus accelerated, honors and advanced placement. Add to those special programs, such as the Puente [Project] for educational enhancement and Advancement Via Individual Determination. I'm not aware of any distinctions between these types of classes being made in data assessment.

Then there are the differences in rigor on grade-level exams. Looking at the California Standards Tests data of these classes, many things become apparent. Ninth graders seem to make the most gains out of any grade level. It's not clear whether the ninth-grade Standardized Testing and Reporting test is easier, or if, developmentally, students make a huge leap between junior high and high school. But it seems as if ninth-grade teachers would be compensated the most simply because they teach ninth grade.

Bonus Pay, Not Salaries

In addition to the problems we face in the classroom, studies have shown that putting the carrot of better pay in front of teachers doesn't necessarily make them teach any better.

Good teachers can't do much better than they're already doing. They're already arriving early, staying late, grading papers all weekend, running after-school tutoring programs. If you told a teacher like this they'd make more if they did more, they'd rightly ask how you expect them to do more.

Even so, I am in favor of giving high-achieving teachers more money. Even if they aren't suddenly going to start working harder, they can still receive a bonus for doing a great job.

This is why we should tie student achievement to bonus pay, not teacher salaries. This is an important distinction, and there are already some programs out there trying this approach.

For example, the Teacher Advancement Program (TAP) has begun a trial in California's Lucia Mar [Unified] School District. Although the program does tie teacher pay to student performance, it is the only such project that does so in the form of bonuses. Our educational system should not be penalizing a teacher's already meager salary.

I have no problem being evaluated and held accountable for the job I'm doing. My door is always open, and I welcome discussions that will hold our profession accountable for teaching the next generation. With the negative perceptions we face, opening the realities of what we do every day for all to see could be a wonderful idea.

But if we want to tie student achievement to teacher pay, let's make sure it isn't the only criterion we use. My ninth graders just put on *Romeo and Juliet* in its entirety. They memorized lines of Shakespeare and delivered stunning soliloquies. I have yet to come across a standardized test that would assess something like this.

So even though it is most likely not being done right, should we still offer bonuses to teachers whose students are most prepared to ace multiple-choice tests? If it means more money for teachers, I have to say yes—and hope we get better at assessing teachers and students in the meantime.

> *"The result of this approach—judging teachers by the score gains of their students—will incentivize teachers to avoid students with the greatest needs."*

Tying Teacher Pay to Test Scores Is Bad Policy

Bernie Froese-Germain

Bernie Froese-Germain is a researcher at the Canadian Teachers' Federation. In the following viewpoint, he argues that tying teacher pay to student test scores is a bad idea. He points out that merit pay systems encourage teachers to compete against one another rather than cooperate. In addition, merit pay programs incentivize teachers to focus on test scores rather than on other measures of student learning. Finally, he says, linking pay to test scores pushes teachers away from the classrooms with the greatest need, where test scores will likely be lowest. He concludes that merit pay does not work and should not be implemented in schools.

Bernie Froese-Germain, "Weighing In on the Teacher Merit Pay Debate," Canadian Teachers' Federation Notes, March 2011. Copyright © 2011 Canadian Teachers' Federation. Reproduced by permission.

As you read, consider the following questions:

1. What controversial step did the *Los Angeles Times* take in regard to teacher performance, according to Froese-Germain?

2. According to Froese-Germain, what learning goals might be displaced by a focus on testing?

3. What lesson does Froese-Germain draw for education policy makers in Canada?

First the good news. There's a growing consensus that the quality of teachers and teaching is a major factor—some would say the most important school-based factor—in the quality of student learning. In sum (and this comes as no surprise to the teaching profession), good teaching matters.

The Rise of Merit Pay

The bad news is that, in this highly charged climate of data-driven accountability, teacher effectiveness and compensation are increasingly being tied to student scores on standardized tests.

For example, the Los Angeles Unified School District is among a growing number of U.S. school districts using the results of standardized tests to determine the "value-added" outcomes produced by the teacher (the value-added measure of teacher performance is related to gains in test scores in the teacher's class over time). Using this data, the *L.A. Times* last summer (2010) published performance ratings for more than 6,000 L.A. elementary teachers, naming and ranking individual teachers as effective or ineffective on the basis of math and reading test scores.

More recently, the New York City Department of Education announced plans to release the value-added measurement (VAM) scores for more than 12,000 public school teachers. A request by the United Federation of Teachers [UFT] to keep the teachers' names confidential has been denied by a Manhattan judge. The UFT intends to appeal the ruling.

A study just published by the National Education Policy Center [NEPC] at the University of Colorado has found serious flaws in the research used to determine the controversial widely reported *L.A. Times* ratings, stating that it was "demonstrably inadequate to support the published rankings." According to the NEPC,

> "This study makes it clear that the *L.A. Times* and its research team have done a disservice to the teachers, students, and parents of Los Angeles. The *Times* owes its community a better accounting for its decision to publish the names and rankings of individual teachers when it knew or should have known that those rankings were based on a questionable analysis. In any case, the *Times* now owes its community an acknowledgment of the tremendous weakness of the results reported and an apology for the damage its reporting has done."

The concept of merit pay tied to test results has gained momentum as a result of the U.S. Race to the Top program. The *New York Times* reports that eleven states have introduced legislation linking "student achievement to teacher evaluations and, in some cases, to pay and job security." All of this is putting pressure on teacher tenure. Since the beginning of 2011, state governors in Florida, Idaho, Indiana, Nevada, and New Jersey have called for the elimination or dismantling of teacher tenure provisions.

Understandably there are concerns about the extent to which these trends will spill over into Canada. B.C. [British Columbia] Liberal leadership candidate Kevin Falcon recently floated the idea of a merit pay system for B.C. teachers, igniting debate across the country.

Teacher Rankings

One option is to define an effective teacher as one who increases student learning as measured by student performance on standardized tests. In 2010 the *Los Angeles Times* itself became news when it published rankings of teachers in Los Angeles Unified School District based on *value-added* test scores. "Value-added" measures attempt to capture the change in student test scores that can be attributed to a particular teacher: By focusing on the change in scores, value-added measures attempt to control for the many other factors that can affect test scores, such as student characteristics. The *LA Times* analysis set off a huge debate in the education community about the use of such measures. Several critics emphasize problems with the measures themselves, particularly the large variability in scores from one year to the next: For example, a teacher could be ranked at the top in one year and at the bottom in the next. Others focus on issues with the underlying tests, arguing that the tests were not designed for the purpose of evaluating teaching and there is more to good teaching than just higher test scores. There are also concerns that tying teacher compensation entirely to test-related measures will create perverse incentives for teachers to cheat and selectively ignore materials and concepts that do not typically appear on standardized tests. Partly because of these concerns, most education analysts prefer using multiple measures; for example, combining value-added scores with classroom observations and evaluations from administrators or peers.

Mark H. Maier and Jennifer Imazeki,
The Data Game: Controversies in Social Science Statistics.
4th ed. New York: Taylor and Francis, 2013.

Undermining Teamwork

Tying teacher evaluation and remuneration to test results is problematic on numerous levels, not least of which it reinforces a competitive spirit that undermines teacher collegiality and teamwork.

Michael Fullan, speaking at Ontario's Building Blocks for Education summit in September 2010, "dismissed merit pay outright as an effective way to motivate teachers."

In an extensive review of the research on merit pay in education and other sectors, Dr. Ben Levin, professor and Canada Research Chair in Education Leadership and Policy at OISE/UT [Ontario Institute for Studies in Education, University of Toronto], argues convincingly that "linking teachers' pay to student achievement is not a desirable education policy" for many reasons:

- Very few people anywhere in the labour force are paid on the basis of measured outcomes.

- No other profession is paid on the basis of measured client outcomes.

- Most teachers oppose such schemes.

- The measurement of merit in teaching inevitably involves a degree of error.

- The details of merit pay schemes vary widely, yet these details have great impact on how such plans are received and their effects on teachers and schools.

- Pay based on student achievement is highly likely to lead to displacement of other important education purposes and goals—on this point Levin stresses that, "when people have a financial incentive to achieve a score, that incentive may displace other, more desirable traits. Quite a bit of research in psychology shows that extrinsic rewards can act to displace intrinsic motivation, in which case merit pay schemes could reduce some teachers' desire to do the job well simply because that is their professional responsibility and wish. Teachers, like other public-sector workers, are primarily motivated by non-financial factors (though of course pay is also relevant)".

- There is no consensus on what the measures of merit should be—according to Levin, "the rationale behind merit pay is to link teachers' pay to student outcomes. However schooling has many outcomes, so the question of which outcomes to use to determine merit is highly problematic. Academic achievement is not the only important outcome of schooling; we also value students' ongoing ability to learn, interest in learning, abilities to work with others, and citizenship skills. Most of these, however, will not be used in any given merit pay scheme because they would make it too complicated."

In addition, merit pay schemes in education have a long record of failure. Levin notes that

merit pay is not a new idea. Such plans go back more than 100 years. There has not, however, been a great deal of careful empirical study. Some of the studies currently cited are from very different contexts, such as India, and may have little applicability to Canada. Studies in developed countries yield equivocal results, but very few have found strong positive effects. Further, though many merit pay schemes have been adopted in various parts of the US in the last 20 years, few of these have lasted more than a few years, suggesting that for one reason or another they were not sustainable. Where evidence is weak and experience is not positive, there are good reasons to be guarded about any policy.

Indeed a recent study by the National Center on Performance Incentives at Vanderbilt University in Nashville, described as "the most rigorous study of performance-based teacher compensation ever conducted in the United States," concluded that merit pay had no overall impact on student achievement. In this three-year trial, teachers in the treatment group received significant bonuses of up to $15,000.

Bad Incentives

And as Diane Ravitch explains, merit pay can also undermine equity in our schools:

> Tests that assess what students have learned are not intended to be, nor are they, measures of teacher quality. It is easier for teachers to get higher test scores if they teach advantaged students. If they teach children who are poor or children who are English language learners, or homeless children, or children with disabilities, they will not get big score gains. So, the result of this approach—judging teachers by the score gains of their students—will incentivize teachers to avoid students with the greatest needs. This is just plain stupid as a matter of policy.

If there's a lesson in all of this for education policy makers in Canada, it is this—merit pay is another in a series of market-based education policy reforms that doesn't stand up to scrutiny, one being driven by ideology rather than sound research.

Periodical and Internet Sources Bibliography

The following articles have been selected to supplement the diverse views presented in this chapter.

Rachel Aviv	"Wrong Answer," *New Yorker*, July 21, 2014.
David Callahan	"Why Teachers Cheat," *Huffington Post*, April 1, 2013.
Jonathan Chait	"Teachers Cheating on Tests: Not a Big Deal," *New York Magazine*, April 2, 2013.
Thomas Kane and Linda Darling-Hammond	"Should Student Test Scores Be Used to Evaluate Teachers?," *Wall Street Journal*, June 24, 2012.
Jason Kelly	"Failed Tests," *University of Chicago Magazine*, January–February 2012.
Ronald A. Lindsay	"We Should Not Evaluate Teachers Based on Student Test Scores," Center for Inquiry, April 15, 2015.
New York Daily News	"Testing, Testing: Union-Organized 'Opt Out' Campaign Against Common Core Exams Protects Teachers, Not Students," April 13, 2015.
Robby Soave	"Earth to Teachers. Come in, Teachers. You Can't Support Common Core but Oppose Testing," Reason.com, October 31, 2014.
Valerie Strauss	"Teacher: I Am Not Against Common Core or Testing—but Here's My Line in the Sand," *Washington Post*, May 1, 2015.
Darrell West	"How Technology Can Stop Cheating," *Huffington Post*, August 20, 2013.
Alia Wong and Terrance F. Ross	"When Teachers Cheat," *Atlantic*, April 2, 2015.

CHAPTER 4

What Are Ethical Issues for Teachers Outside the Classroom?

Chapter Preface

In 2010 Melissa Petro, an elementary school art teacher in New York, wrote an article for *Huffington Post* in which she talked about having worked as a stripper and a prostitute before she became a teacher. After these revelations, she was suspended and eventually forced to resign. Mayor Michael Bloomberg himself called for her removal. "Friday night when I was informed that, of the situation of this teacher saying that she had been a sex worker—I think was the term she might have used—I said 'well, you know, call her, tell her that she is being removed from the classroom,'" Bloomberg was quoted as saying in a *New York Daily News* article.

Bloomberg's comments do not really explain his reasoning or what danger he thought Petro posed to children. Why is it a moral imperative to keep strippers or sex workers from teaching in elementary school? And is it ethical to fire teachers because of their previous jobs, even when those teachers (like Petro) have tenure?

Ruth Graham, writing at the Grindstone website argues that it was ethical to fire Petro, not because of her former job but because she had written about that job so publicly. Graham argues that Petro had the right to write about her work. However, Graham says, the First Amendment "doesn't guarantee you'll never experience political or social consequences of exercising those rights." Graham also says that Petro's decision to enter sex work was a choice, and that "the more I see Petro's entry into stripping and prostitution as a choice, the less sympathy I have when she experiences the totally predictable consequences of that choice."

Petro herself in an article for *Salon*, explains why she entered sex work, and why she decided to talk about it in public.

> I didn't think my story would be shocking . . . because, well, my story *isn't* shocking. Whereas some women's road to sex

work entails coercion and last-ditch survival, for me, this wasn't the case. The product of a working-class home—the first in her family to go to college, let alone study abroad—my working as a stripper began as a means to an end. Prior to stripping, I'd worked in fast food. I'd worked in retail. I even spent one summer delivering singing telegrams. I was used to long hours, unreasonable bosses and very little pay; stripping—at least at first—was the ideal job.

Petro explains that she ended up deciding that sex work was not right for her, in part because it was so stigmatized that she had to lie about what she was doing to friends and family. Eventually, she moved into teaching, which she loved. However, she says, "My past had no bearing on my competence as a teacher, and so I refused to operate as if it did. The idea that an elementary school teacher wasn't entitled to a life in her off-hours I found equally absurd."

Petro, herself, decided sex work was not for her and so got another job. Then officials decided that her sex work disqualified her for other jobs. The logic seems to prevent sex workers from getting other employment; this makes it difficult, and in some cases impossible, for individuals to stop doing sex work. This does not seem like an ethical outcome.

The following chapter examines other ethical issues involving teachers outside the classroom, including teachers' use of social media, teachers' friendships with students, and professors dating students in a college setting.

> *"Should teachers use social media? Yes ... however, they need to realize that their vocation brings certain responsibilities with it."*

Ethically, Teachers Must Restrict Their Speech on Social Media

Joseph M. Yeager

Joseph M. Yeager is a writer for Newsmax and an adjunct professor. In the following viewpoint, he argues that teachers should be very aware of the dangers of social media use and should restrict their speech accordingly. Teachers should be allowed to use social media, he says, but they should be aware that pictures showing them acting inappropriately or posts about their students are public and that they may face repercussions. Yeager says that teachers should not "friend" students on social media, as this disrupts the student-teacher relationship and is unprofessional. Teachers, he concludes, should be circumspect in sharing information on social media.

Joseph M. Yeager, MBA, "Should Teachers Use Social Media?," Montcojoe.wix.com (blog). October 13, 2015. http://montcojoe.wix.com/josephmyeager Copyright © 2015 Joseph M. Yeager. Reproduced by permission.

As you read, consider the following questions:

1. What platforms are more popular with students than Facebook, according to Yeager?

2. What three things does Yeager recommend for teachers to protect themselves on social media?

3. A teacher in Yeager's district was fired in 2012 for what reason?

While some people do not have to consider their job when it comes to what they post on social media, teachers are in a somewhat unique position. As an educator myself, this is something that I have to consider pretty carefully. In my case, I am an adjunct faculty member for a local university. That is still very different from teachers of preschool to 12th-grade students. In their case, it may not even be a question of what they should or should not post onto a social media account but should they even be using social media at all.

Only you can decide if social media is the right thing for you. There are benefits and risks associated with using social media for everyone; even more so for teachers. Before deciding, however, there are some issues that need to be addressed. What I will do here is address some of those issues and then review some of the social media platforms and review how they can impact you, both personally and professionally.

Should Teachers Be on Social Media at All?

This is a tough one. Just by having a social media account, teachers open themselves up to a variety of issues. Most social media sites have privacy settings that help prevent others from seeing what you post online. It is important to realize that I said "help" prevent and not "will" prevent. Despite the most stringent privacy settings available, it can all come undone if even one of your online friends shares your content onto their own account. Your privacy settings are only as strong as your weakest link!

Also consider that even if you teach at a primary school, where students should be too young to use sites such as Facebook, that does not prevent their parents from seeing what is on your account. The principal at my daughter's elementary school closed her Facebook account after parents saw pictures of her enjoying a drink while on vacation. It was a single drink, but people started asking if it was appropriate behavior. I know this woman well and have the utmost trust in her and in her ability. She is an excellent principal.

Assuming that you decide to use social media, which platform(s) are best for you? With over 1 billion users, clearly Facebook is the leader in social media. It's where your friends and family probably are, and if you want to share updates with them, you'll want to be there, too. Of course, it's likely that many of your students and their families will be there, too.

Despite many stories about how kids are leaving Facebook, the reality is that they're not leaving it altogether; they're simply using it less as they migrate to other platforms, such as Snapchat, Instagram, Vine, etc. All of these sites provide a faster-paced environment, which appeals to younger generations, but they can and do continue to use Facebook.

If you think that LinkedIn is kid free, you should know that last year, LinkedIn lowered its minimum age requirement from 18 to 14. . . . And again, even if you don't run into your students on LinkedIn, you still run the risk of running into a parent. I'm not suggesting that you shouldn't use the site, but I want you to understand the reality of the situation, including the risks.

Another issue facing teachers is that there has been an increase in the number of incidents where students have actually cyberbullied their teachers.

Should I "Friend" My Students?

In my opinion, this is a no-brainer. The answer is no. Teachers are held to a higher standard than people in many other professions; for good reason. By friending students, it can lead to a breakdown of the teacher-student relationship. Even at the college level, I require that my students do not use my first name. Imagine how students might interpret being your "friend," even if it is online. If you've ever read Tony Danza's book about teaching at Northeast High School in Philadelphia, it's a school policy that students are not allowed to address teachers by their first name.

Even the hint of inappropriate behavior can destroy a teacher's hard-earned reputation and career. Last, Carol Thebarge, a teacher in New Hampshire, was fired from her position because she had friended students via social media. She had over 250 students as friends on Facebook. As this was against the school's policy, she was asked to unfriend them. When she refused, the school district terminated her. Despite support from many in her community, even if she was offered her position back, Thebarge has indicated that she would not accept it.

Similar to friending students is if you should connect/friend their parents? Again, I say that the answer is no. This can become a bit trickier, as you may have been friends with them even before their kids started going to your school, particularly in a smaller town/school district. That applies to any social media platform, such as LinkedIn or Twitter also.

If you do use social media, be sure to check your school/district's policy regarding social media. For any organization looking to create a social media policy for its employees, I always recommend Chris Boudreaux's site: Social Media Governance.

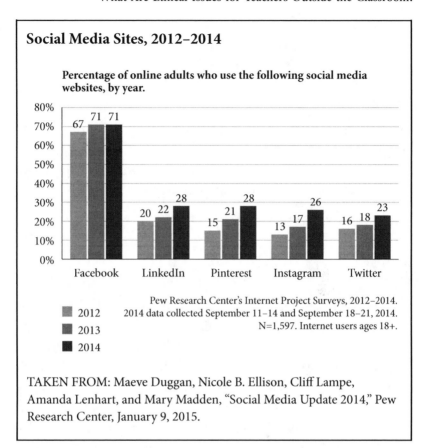

Social Media Sites, 2012–2014

Percentage of online adults who use the following social media websites, by year.

Pew Research Center's Internet Project Surveys, 2012–2014.
2014 data collected September 11–14 and September 18–21, 2014.
N=1,597. Internet users ages 18+.

TAKEN FROM: Maeve Duggan, Nicole B. Ellison, Cliff Lampe, Amanda Lenhart, and Mary Madden, "Social Media Update 2014," Pew Research Center, January 9, 2015.

Legal Considerations

Many employers conduct background checks prior to hiring someone. More frequently, this includes potential employees' social media. As the *New York Law Journal* reports, "there are no laws that prohibit the use of social media to screen or recruit applicants." That means that school districts can view your social media accounts and see what you have posted.

It also means that they can only see what you make available to the general public. They do not have the right to demand that you provide them with your passwords so that they can see what you have hidden behind your privacy settings and other content, such as private messages that are not visible to the general public. According to the Equal Employment Opportunity Commission, only four states have passed laws that specifically forbid employers from requiring a person to provide this information.

Protecting Yourself

When using social media, teachers must employ some commonsense techniques to keep their private life separate from their work life. As I wrote on another site, there are three easy things that you can do to help protect yourself:

- Minimize your digital footprint

- Regularly check your accounts' privacy settings

- Improve password management

Too many people fail to minimize their digital footprint, perhaps because they naively think that nothing bad will happen to them. Beyond the issue of cyberbullying, making too much information available on your profile can help facilitate identity theft. I've seen people provide their name, address, birthday, phone number and more on their Facebook page. That's way too much! Additionally, they left it open for the entire world to see by not adjusting their privacy settings—another big mistake. . . .

I consider these three steps actions that everyone, not just teachers, should take into account when using social media. Too often, people place a virtual bull's-eye on themselves and the repercussions can be more far-reaching than they expect—not just for themselves, but for their friends and family!

Answering the First Question

I never did answer the first question that I posed here: should teachers use social media? Yes, I believe that they should be allowed to use it if they wish to do so, however, they need to realize that their vocation brings certain responsibilities with it. Just as a teacher could expect to face repercussions if they were intoxicated in public or any other questionable behavior, what they do online and who they interact with online is a major issue that they need to consider before doing so.

By following the three recommendations from the previous section, people can minimize the risks associated with using social media. Again, I did not say avoid or eliminate the risks because the only way to do that is to not use social media.

A teacher in my own county was fired in 2012 because of comments she made on her blog, where she called her students "disengaged, lazy whiners." I remember when the story broke; there was little support for her in the community. That's not to say that people did not empathize with her, but they were amazed that she would actually post her comments in such a public manner.

| *"The jobs one has determines the civil rights one has."*

Restricting Teachers' Speech on Social Media Is Ethically Dangerous

Ilana Gershon

Ilana Gershon is an associate professor in the Department of Communication and Culture at Indiana University. In the following viewpoint, she says that teachers are policed and sometimes fired based on their social media statements. She says that free speech protections have been qualified by the Supreme Court, which has said that employers have the right to fire employees for speech when the individual speaks as an employee. Teachers who anger students or parents through social media posts are seen as alienating customers of the school system, and so are subject to discipline. Gershon concludes that this trend is eroding free speech for all employees and especially for teachers.

As you read, consider the following questions:

1. According to Gershon, what did the Supreme Court decide in *Garcetti et al. v. Ceballos*?

Ilana Gershon, "Don't Post So Close to Me," *The Hooded Utilitarian*, January 6, 2014. Hoodedutilitarian.com. Copyright © 2014 The Hooded Utilitarian. Reproduced by permission.

2. How is new media involved in cases of sexual harassment involving teachers, according to Gershon?

3. How did a principal get access to the teacher's Facebook post in the 2011 case in New Jersey, even though the teacher had made her settings private, according to the viewpoint?

As neoliberal [that is, market-based] logics enter more and more institutions, what it means to have civil rights may be gradually shifting. In her introduction to *Ethnographies of Neoliberalism*, Carol [J.] Greenhouse has pointed out that under neoliberal logics, the language of rights is increasingly used to sustain markets. Yet as anyone who has paid attention to recent arguments about government surveillance and privacy [knows], it is not only the language of rights that is used to sustain markets. The very concept of rights is being revised to sustain markets, even in cases that seem too minor to require this imposition of neoliberal logic, such as when courts decide cases of wrongful dismissal. There is a category of person that in the United States has become one of the canaries in the coal mines for this process—K–12 public school teachers. There is an increasing number of U.S. legal cases involving wrongful dismissal that address how teachers use new media. I am interested in how courts deal with the fact that teaching, along with many other jobs, is the kind of job in which sometimes teachers complain about their students and about the job itself. Teachers sometimes say things about their six-year-old students such as "I am not a teacher—I am a warden for future criminals!" Teachers have been saying such things for many years, often wearily in their living rooms or a bit furtively in the school parking lot, having looked around first to make sure that there is no one who can overhear. Since 2006, they have also been typing such statements into their status updates on Facebook. When teachers do this on Facebook in the United States, it turns out that they risk being fired. "My students are the future criminals of America," or some such utterance, apparently is not something a teacher who wishes to remain a teacher says using new media. And sometimes, after the school system fires them, they or the union representing them, will sue, often pointing out that teachers are citizens, and saying unkind things about one's students should be protected as a matter of free speech. In short, these legal cases are moments in which the U.S. courts reflect upon what it means to speak like a public school teacher and adjudicate whether one's First Amendment rights have or have not been violated because of one's employment status.

Politicizing Education

Why teachers? I think that there are a couple of reasons why teachers and their utterances have become a focus of attention in the contemporary moment. First, teachers, because of the nature of their jobs, are constantly having to negotiate the unsettling properties of new media. They are constantly interacting with school administrators, fellow teachers, parents and students, all of whom have their own informal solutions to the communicative dilemmas that new media can pose to communities of users. Teachers are continually engaging with differently structured audiences, and often doing so using technologies that erase the boundaries between audiences—either literally merging audiences as Facebook's interface often does or through the ever increasing ease of circulating words, as in the technological infrastructure of email and cell phones that enable people to forward emails and text messages so quickly and effortlessly.

At the same time, in the United States at the moment there is an ongoing effort by politicians and government bureaucrats to privatize education. Those funding education have increasingly been arguing that market-based solutions provide the best and most effective strategies to educate students. This involves breaking teachers' unions, which are seen as preventing these market-based solutions and protecting inept teachers. The cases that come before the court are often cases in which teachers had tenure and so were able to sue the school districts for wrongful dismissal, although there is in fact one case in which a teacher's contract was simply not being renewed, supposedly for a rather turgid political poem he posted on Myspace months earlier. In short, by looking at teachers, I am turning to a moment in which audit culture meets the surveillance society.

Restricting Employee Speech

This intersection has become particularly acute since 2006, when the U.S. Supreme Court ruled in *Garcetti [et al.] v. Ceballos* that a public employee's free speech is not protected under the Constitution, although a citizen's free speech is. [Richard] Ceballos, a deputy district attorney in Los Angeles, believed that there were substantial errors in an affidavit used to convince a judge to issue a search warrant. He wrote a memo suggesting that the criminal case be dropped and ended up testifying in court after being subpoenaed by the defense counsel. He then faced what he considered retaliation at work for doing so—he was demoted, his cases were transferred to other, less experienced colleagues, and he was barred from handling any future murder cases. The Supreme Court ruled that the salient question was whether Ceballos spoke as a public employee or a citizen, and in this instance, it was clear that he spoke as a public employee. As a public employee, he was not guaranteed protection under the First Amendment; his rights to free speech were only protected when he spoke as a citizen. With this ruling, the Supreme Court overturned 42 years of court decisions that had declared a public employee's speech was in fact protected; now one's job could determine what one was allowed to say. And subsequent relevant court cases reflect this change, as the decisions now tend to revolve

The Supreme Court on Employee Speech

Respondent [Richard] Ceballos, a supervising deputy district attorney, was asked by defense counsel to review a case in which, counsel claimed, the affidavit police used to obtain a critical search warrant was inaccurate. Concluding after the review that the affidavit made serious misrepresentations, Ceballos relayed his findings to his supervisors, petitioners here, and followed up with a disposition memorandum recommending dismissal. Petitioners nevertheless proceeded with the prosecution. At a hearing on a defense motion to challenge the warrant, Ceballos recounted his observations about the affidavit, but the trial court rejected the challenge. Claiming that petitioners then retaliated against him for his memo in violation of the First and Fourteenth Amendments, Ceballos filed a 42 U.S.C. §1983 suit. The district court granted petitioners summary judgment, ruling, *inter alia*, that the memo was not protected speech because Ceballos wrote it pursuant to his employment duties. Reversing, the Ninth Circuit held that the memo's allegations were protected under the First Amendment analysis in *Pickering v. Board of Ed. of Township High School Dist. 205, Will Cty.*, 391 U.S. 563, and *Connick v. Myers*, 461 U.S. 138.

Garcetti et al. v. Ceballos, *Legal Information Institute, Cornell University Law School, May 30, 2006.*

around how to define the defendant—as a citizen, public employee or simply employee. Other critical legal scholars have pointed out that this decision is extending a neoliberal logic by allowing employers to circumscribe someone's rights to free speech when they define a position's responsibilities. In these cases, one's right to free speech is determined by one's manager's definition of the job. And this is in the background when courts decide cases about how teachers can use new media.

There are two primary ways in which new media is involved when teachers are fired. The first, and still most common situation, is when a teacher inappropriately sleeps with or sexually harasses a student or coworker. In these cases, free speech is not an issue. The case revolves around whether or not the sexual misconduct did in fact take place. The court decision will mention people's new media use, and primarily will discuss with some detail the frequency of contact between the teacher and student or coworker. *[State of] Tennessee v. [Sandy L.] Binkley*: "Those records indicated that the Defendant and C.B. exchanged messages with one another 841 times between March 10, 2008, and September 23, 2008, with some of those texts occurring as late as 1:00 A.M." Frequency and time of communication here is part and parcel of court evidence of inappropriate interactions. In these cases, it is the relationship between the teacher and defendant and others that is at issue, and their use of a particular medium is relevant only inasmuch as the medium itself can enable police to trace how often and when contact was made.

But teachers also post things on Facebook or Myspace in which the utterance itself is considered the reason for firing someone; it is violation enough in itself, not merely a trace of other inappropriate practices. I want to turn to a case in north New Jersey that received quite a bit of media attention as well. In late March 2011, a teacher posted as a Facebook status update the following: "I'm not a teacher—I'm a warden for future criminals! They had a scared straight program in school—why couldn't i [sic] bring 1st graders?" The Scared Straight program brings former inmates to talk to students who are 12 years old or older at schools, so when the teacher mentions being a warden, she is also implicitly referring to the program that took place at her school. In the hearing, the teacher explains her word choice in these terms. She had set up privacy settings for her Facebook profile, so only her 300 Facebook friends could see this status update. Her then principal was not one of her Facebook friends, but her former principal was. When her former boss saw the status update, he decided to contact her current principal by email, explaining he was troubled by the post and cutting and pasting her status update into his email message. Her current principal then found a way to print out a copy of the actual Facebook profile and update before meeting with the teacher and asking, "What were you thinking?" After suspending her, news of her Facebook post circulated among parents and students, sparking a wave of protests. Her comments were interpreted as racist, in part because she had recently been transferred from another more affluent school to a poorer school where her first grade class was entirely comprised of African American and Latino students. She had never been reprimanded before, but because of this Facebook post, she was dismissed. She was a tenured teacher, and so when she sued, claiming wrongful dismissal, her case went before an administrative law judge.

Speaking like a Teacher

The judge's decision reveals a deep concern with how best to conceptualize the role from which the teacher typed, as well as a critique of the teacher's presentation of self, and in particular, of contrition. The judge describes at some length the ways in which the teacher apologizes, and why her words and lack of emotion did not count as a proper apology. The teacher seems to hold a different media ideology than the judge. The judge writes: "At the hearing, [the teacher] seemed still unable to genuinely understand why her Facebook posts had engendered such an extreme reaction. But she disagreed with [the principal's] testimony that she did not apologize to him. [The teacher] stated that she told [the principal] that she was 'very sorry that this caused trouble.' I offered [the teacher] an opportunity to elaborate on the reasons for her remorse by asking her why she apologized to [the principal]. [The teacher] reiterated that it was because she 'was sorry for any fuss' her Facebook post created, and for the problems it created for her principal and herself." The judge finds this apology unsatisfying, and later in her decision explains what the teacher should say—what a good teacher must utter in these circumstances: "If this was an aberrational lapse in judgment, a reaction to an unusually bad day, I would have expected to have heard more genuine and passionate contrition in [the teacher's] testimony. I needed to hear that she was terribly sorry she had insulted her young students; that she loved being their teacher; and that she wanted desperately to return to the classroom. I heard nothing of the sort. Rather, I came away with the impression that [the teacher] remained somewhat befuddled by the commotion she had created, and that while she continued to maintain that her conduct was not inappropriate, she was sorry others thought differently." In sum, it is not only [the teacher's] Facebook posts that demonstrate she does not understand the correct ways to speak as a teacher, it is also her performance in the hearing—she continues to refuse to perform her role as a concerned and caring teacher properly according to the judge.

The judge is then faced with a dilemma—how best to explain that a Facebook post is not an issue of free speech. And here she resorts to a neoliberal argument to explain why free speech is not a relevant principle here. She argues that the teacher is like any other employee, obligated to the school as her employer to treat her customers well—and in this case the students and parents are defined as the customers. Businesses are supposed to be protected by law from employees' rude speech to customers, and the judge determines that this Facebook posting violates this legal protection, and so the teacher can be legally dismissed.

Policing Speech

These court cases become moments in which what it means to speak like a teacher are being both evaluated and policed. For the most part, when teachers speak in ways their schools and local communities judge inappropriate, these are dilemmas resolved more informally by principals and school boards. Courts are less frequently involved. However, the court cases themselves have a larger impact; teachers and prospective teachers have started policing their own new media presence. They are gradually realizing that their comments on social media are not only scrutinized but can be a basis for dismissal. They become more and more aware that their individual understanding of how a particular medium structures what is or is not public speech must give way to a larger societal perception of what counts as public speech and what counts as private speech. In the process, they come to realize that the jobs one has determines the civil rights one has, that one's relationship vis-à-vis business defines one's speech far more than one's relationship as a citizen vis-à-vis the state.

| "I see no good reason to offer a permanent faculty position to someone whose discourse crosses the line into anti-Semitism."

It Is Ethical for Colleges to Punish Teachers for Comments on Social Media

Cary Nelson

Cary Nelson served as national president of the American Association of University Professors from 2006 to 2012. He teaches at the University of Illinois at Urbana-Champaign. In the following viewpoint, he discusses Steven Salaita, a professor who was promised a position at the University of Illinois but was subsequently denied the post because of his angry tweets against the Israeli occupation of Palestine. Nelson argues that Salaita's tweets were inflammatory and showed him to be intolerant, anti-Semitic, and a poor potential colleague. Nelson also worries that Jewish students would be afraid to voice opinions in Salaita's classes. He concludes that there are good academic reasons not to hire Salaita and says that the decision to reject him was the right one.

Cary Nelson, "An Appointment to Reject," *Inside Higher Ed*, August 8, 2014. Insidehighered.com. Copyright © 2014 Inside Higher Ed. Reproduced by permission.

As you read, consider the following questions:

1. According to the viewpoint, why does Nelson follow the work of Salaita?

2. Why does Nelson say that this is not a matter of academic freedom, and under what circumstances would it become one in his view?

3. Cite two or three of Salaita's inflammatory tweets mentioned by Nelson.

This month [August 2014], my campus, the University of Illinois at Urbana-Champaign, was widely expected to welcome Steven Salaita as a new faculty member. He was to be a tenured professor in the American Indian Studies program. But a decision not to present the appointment to the Board of Trustees was made by the chancellor. Although I was not involved in the process and did not communicate my views to the administration, I want to say why I believe the decision not to offer him a job was the right one.

Inflammatory Tweets

Salaita has written credibly on fiction by Arab Americans and is, so I am told, knowledgeable about Native American studies. But Salaita's national profile—and the basis of his aspirations to being a public intellectual—is entirely based on his polemical interventions in debates over the Arab/Israeli conflict. Those interventions include his 2011 book *Israel's Dead Soul*, which I read last year, and his widely quoted and prolific tweeting. *Israel's Dead Soul* is published by Temple University Press, so it is part of his academic profile. His tweets cover precisely the same territory. This more public side of his persona would be widely available to his students; indeed his tweets would be better known to students than his scholarly publications. His inflammatory tweets are already being widely read. I have been following his tweets for some months because I have been writing about the Israeli/Palestinian conflict and co-editing a collection of essays titled *The Case Against Academic Boycotts of Israel.* I try to follow the work of all prominent pro-boycott leaders, Salaita among them.

Although I find many of his tweets quite loathsome—as well as sophomoric and irresponsible—I would defend without qualification his right to issue most of them. Academic freedom protects him from university reprisals for his extramural speech, unless he appears to be inciting violence, which one retweeted remark that a well-known American reporter wrote a story that "should have ended at the pointy end of a shiv" appears to do. His June 19 [2014] response to the kidnapping of three Israeli teenagers—"You may be too refined to say it, but I'm not: I wish all the f------ West Bank settlers would go missing"—also invokes a violent response to the occupation, since "go missing" refers to kidnapping.

Salaita and Collegiality

But his right to make most of these statements does not mean I would choose to have him as a colleague. His tweets are the sordid underbelly, the more frank and revealing counterpart, to his more extended arguments about Middle Eastern history and the Israeli/Palestinian conflict. They are likely to shape his role on campus when 2015's Israeli Apartheid Week rolls around. I am told he can be quite charismatic in person, so he may deploy his tweeting rhetoric at public events on campus. Faculty members are well within their rights to evaluate someone as a potential colleague and to consider what contributions a candidate might make to the campus community. It is the whole Salaita package that defines in the end the desirability and appropriateness of offering him a faculty appointment.

I should add that this is not an issue of academic freedom. If Salaita were a faculty member here and he were being sanctioned for his public statements, it would be. But a campus and its faculty members have the right to consider whether, for example, a job candidate's publications, statements to the press, social media presence, public lectures, teaching profile, and so forth suggest he or she will make a positive contribution to the department, student life, and the community as a whole. Here at Illinois, even the department head who would have appointed Salaita agreed in *Inside Higher Ed* that "any public statement that someone makes is fair game for consideration." Had Salaita already signed a contract, then of course he would have to have received full due process, including a full hearing, before his prospective offer could be withdrawn. But my understanding is that he had not received a contract.

Salaita condenses boycott-divestment-sanctions [BDS] wisdom into a continuing series of sophomoric, bombastic, or anti-Semitic tweets: "UCSCdivest passes. Mark Yudoff nervously twirls his two remaining hairs, puts in an angry call to Janet Napolitano" (May 28, 2014); "10,000 students at USF [University of South Florida] call for divestment. The university dismisses it out of hand. That's Israel-style democracy" (May 28, 2014); "Somebody just told me F.W. DeKlerk doesn't believe Israel is an apartheid state. This is what Zionists have been reduced to" (May 28, 2014); "All of Israel's hand-wringing about demography leads one to only one reasonable conclusion: Zionists are ineffective lovers" (May 26, 2014); "Universities are filled with faculty and admins whose primary focus is policing criticism of Israel that exceeds their stringent preferences" (May 25, 2014); "'Israel army' and 'moral code' go together like polar bears and rainforests" (May 25, 2014); "Keep BDS going! The more time Israel spends on it, the fewer resources it can devote to pillaging and plundering" (May 23, 2014); "So, how long will it be before the Israeli government starts dropping white phosphorous on American college campuses?" (May 23, 1014); "Even the most tepid overture to Palestinian humanity can result in Zionist histrionics" (May 21, 2014); "All life is sacred. Unless you're a Zionist, for whom most life is a mere inconvenience to ethnographic supremacy" (May 20, 2014); "I fully expect the Israeli soldiers who murdered two teens in cold blood to receive a commendation or promotion" (May 20, 2014); "Understand that whenever a Zionist frets about Palestinian violence, it is a projection of his own brute psyche" (May 20, 2014); "I don't want to hear another damn word about 'nonviolence.' Save it for Israel's child-killing soldiers" (May 19, 2014); "I stopped listening at 'dialogue'" (May 27, 2014). The last example here presumably advises BDS students how interested they should be in conversations with people holding different views.

More recently he has said, "if [Benjamin] Netanyahu appeared on TV with a necklace made from the teeth of Palestinian children, would anyone be surprised" (July 19, 2014) and "By eagerly conflating Jewishness and Israel, Zionists are partly responsible when people say anti-Semitic shit in response to Israeli terror" (July 18, 2014). The following day, he offered a definition: "Zionists: transforming 'anti-Semitism' from something horrible into something honorable since 1948" (July 19).

Student Discomfort

It is remarkable that a senior faculty member chooses to present himself in public this way. Meanwhile, the mix of deadly seriousness, vehemence, and low comedy in this appeal to students is genuinely unsettling. Will Jewish students in his classes feel comfortable after they read "Let's cut to the chase: If you're defending Israel right now you're an awful human being" (July 8), "Zionist uplift in America: every little Jewish boy and girl can grow up to be the leader of a murderous colonial regime" (July 14), or "No wonder Israel prefers killing Palestinians from the sky. It turns out American college kids aren't very good at ground combat" (July 23)? The last of these tweets obviously disparages the two young American volunteers who lost their lives fighting with the Israel Defense Forces in Gaza. What would he say if the Arab/Israeli conflict were to come up in a class he was teaching on Arab American fiction? Would he welcome dissent to his views? Would students believe him if he appeared to do so? As Salaita says of his opposition in an accusation better applied to himself, he has found in Twitter "the perfect medium" in which to "dispense slogans in order to validate collective self-righteousness" (May 14, 2014).

An Academic Decision

While universities need to study all positions on an issue, even the most outrageous ones, I see no good reason to offer a permanent faculty position to someone whose discourse crosses the line into anti-Semitism. I also do not believe this was a political decision. There are many opponents of Israeli policy on the faculty here and many faculty as well who publicly or privately support the boycott movement. If some faculty expressed their view to the chancellor that Salaita's recent tweets—tweets published long after the search committee made its recommendation—justify not making the appointment, they had a right to do so. I believe this was an academic, not a political, decision. Were I to have evidence to the contrary, my view would be different. I regret that the decision was not made until the summer, but then many of the most disturbing of Salaita's tweets did not go online until the summer of 2014, no doubt provoked by events. That is the time frame in which the statements in question were made. That alone made this an exceptional case. I do not think it would have been responsible for the university to have ignored the evolving character of his public profile. For all these reasons I agree that Salaita's appointment is one that should not have been made.

> *"The board attempted to hide these financial motives behind the notion of 'civility' and of protecting students from wayward ideas couched in unappealing language. As I have shown, that is a bogus argument."*

Why the 'Unhiring' of Steven Salaita Is a Threat to Academic Freedom

David Palumbo-Liu

David Palumbo-Liu is the Louise Hewlett Nixon Professor at Stanford University. His most recent book is The Deliverance of Others: Reading Literature in a Global Age. *In the following viewpoint, Palumbo-Liu discusses the case of Steven Salaita, whose job offer from the University of Illinois at Urbana-Champaign was rescinded after Salaita wrote pro-Palestinian, anti-Israel tweets. Palumbo-Liu says that the university board's decision to rescind the offer seems to have been influenced by*

David Palumbo-Liu, "Why the 'Unhiring' of Steven Salaita Is a Threat to Academic Freedom," From *The Nation*, August 27, 2014 © 2014 The Nation Company, LLC. All rights reserved. Used by permission and protected by the Copyright Laws of the United States. The printing, copying, redistribution, or retransmission of this Content without express written permission is prohibited.

threats from donors. He also notes that the decision was made without consultation with faculty members, who are supposed to make academic decisions in universities. Palumbo-Liu concludes that the rescinding of the offer is a threat to the tradition of faculty governance and to academic free speech on controversial issues.

As you read, consider the following questions:

1. According to Palumbo-Liu, how do Salaita's teaching evaluations refute the board's reasoning for "unhiring" him?

2. What is the mission, or responsibility, of a university's board of trustees, according to the viewpoint?

3. What does Palumbo-Liu say is especially "malicious" about the board's actions and reasoning concerning Salaita?

In early August [2014], *Inside Higher Ed* ran a story that sent a shock wave through the academy. It reported that at the University of Illinois at Urbana-Champaign [UIUC], an official offer of a tenured professorial appointment had been rescinded by a top administrative officer. That alone would have been unusual, but concerns grew after sources close to the decision-making process reported that Chancellor Phyllis Wise was responding to calls and emails about Professor Steven Salaita's acerbic and emphatic anti-Israel tweets.

Civility and Academic Freedom

Once scholars heard of this, protests erupted. Within hours, nearly 2,000 signatures were gathered criticizing the decision; now the count is 17,000, and 3,000 professors are now boycotting UIUC. The American Association of University Professors issued a statement declaring that social media expression is private and protected speech and that the use of "civility" as a litmus test—which the university now admits it has done in rescinding the hire of Salaita—is also not acceptable. The former is protected by the First Amendment, and the latter is not only an entirely vague and unmeasurable concept, but denying employment based on an alleged lack of "civility" narrows the wide range of expression and opinion upon which universities and colleges rely.

The University of Illinois board of trustees has now spoken on this case, echoing and giving support to Chancellor Wise's decision. The board insists that speech is not entirely free:

> Our campuses must be safe harbors where students and faculty from all backgrounds and cultures feel valued, respected and comfortable expressing their views. . . .
>
> Disrespectful and demeaning speech that promotes malice is not an acceptable form of civil argument if we wish to ensure that students, faculty and staff are comfortable in a place of scholarship and education. If we educate a generation of students to believe otherwise, we will have jeopardized the very system that so many have made such great sacrifices to defend. There can be no place for that in our democracy, and therefore, there will be no place for it in our university.

In so doing, the board seems to be evoking one of the basic principles of liberal doctrine as set forth by John Stuart Mill: "The only purpose for which power can be rightfully exercised over any member of a civilized community, against his will, is to prevent harm to others."

There are three important issues to be considered here—and each one reveals the weakness and duplicity of the trustees' decision. As we move through them, we see that this case reflects two disturbing trends: a campaign to silence critics of Israel and the undermining of faculty governance at American universities in favor of corporate control.

Faculty Governance in Danger

Following the end of the Civil War . . . a system of "shared governance" that gave an increasingly professionalized faculty a significant role in academic decision making arose as a crucial element in the development of the modern American university. By the middle of the twentieth century, functioning largely within a context of a growing consensus over the value of shared governance, American higher education gained a position of preeminence in the world. That preeminence was made possible not only by the unparalleled resources that postwar America was able to devote to higher education but also by the development of the system of shared governance and academic freedom that prevailed at America's leading institutions of higher learning. The twin pillars of shared governance and academic freedom helped to support an environment that was both hospitable to scholars seeking to create new knowledge and intellectually challenging for the unprecedented number of students who began entering college after World War Two.

Today, however, the system of shared governance in which faculty have played a significant role in academic decision making is being challenged by critics who argue that more businesslike methods are necessary so that American colleges and universities can be more "flexible" and "nimble" in responding to changing market demands and new technologies.

Larry G. Gerber,
The Rise and Decline of Faculty Governance:
Professionalization and the Modern American University.
Baltimore, MD: John Hopkins University Press, 2014.

Criticism of Israel

First, universities are increasingly being asked to shut down criticism of Israel. This was indeed so with the Salaita case. As I have written elsewhere, some groups have attempted to use Title VI of the 1964 Civil Rights Act to wage legal battles against pro-boycott and pro-divestment protesters, precisely on the grounds that those protests "threatened" Jewish students. But in a determination letter to the University of California, Berkeley, the Department of Education [DOE]:

> found that the kinds of protest events that were the basis of complaint "constitute expression on matters of public concern directed to the university community. In the university environment, exposure to such robust and discordant expressions, *even when personally offensive and hurtful* [emphasis added] is a circumstance that a reasonable student in higher education may experience."

Thus the very founding premise of the UIUC board's decision is disarmed by the DOE finding. Had it cared to, the board might have investigated the history and results of such complaints. But it had other priorities.

Second, a review of Salaita's teaching evaluations at Virginia Tech, a standard part of any hiring process, reveals absolutely no evidence of intimidation, threats or stifling of student opinion. None. Instead, the record shows strong and enthusiastic appreciation of Salaita's teaching and interactions with students. According to this report, the student evaluations for Salaita are spectacular. Repeatedly, he was given near perfect "excellent" scores for "knowledge of subject"; the lowest rating he ever received in the "excellent" category for "overall rating" was 86 percent. It is especially important to note student evaluations of Professor Salaita in the category of "concern and respect" for students. Here too the evaluations are near perfect. The *worst* score was in a class of 28 students. Twenty-five rated him "excellent," two "good," with one no response.

Hence the trustees' decision is based entirely on a hypothetical connection between his allegedly offensive tweets and his potential to harm students. If we assume they discharged their duty and actually read Salaita's file, then they clearly dismissed positive evidence and plowed ahead toward a predetermined conclusion. But even if they did not discharge their duty and read the file, why did they not at least bother to convene an investigatory committee? Here we get to the third issue, which takes us out of the area of stifling criticism of Israel and into much broader, and troubling, territory. The chancellor and board of trustees at UIUC have broken a basic covenant with their faculty. It is a complete misnomer to call this a "university" decision. These administrators may act "on behalf" of the university, but they are not *the* university. And in acting on behalf of the university, it is customary for there to be regular interaction among faculty, administrators and boards of trustees.

Faculty Governance

Faculty governance is the mainstay of the educational process. Faculty are in charge of what goes on in the classroom and who is hired to teach. All hiring decisions are driven by the faculty, and all candidates go through a rigorous process of vetting by a number of faculty committees. Administrators do precisely that—they administer, and should act on faculty appointments only if they determine there has been a flaw in the process.

In the case of dismissing a faculty member, the statutes of the University of Illinois mandate that an investigatory process be followed: "Campus procedures shall include, at a minimum, notice and opportunity for a hearing before the campus provost or equivalent officers or the provost's or equivalent officer's designee." There was absolutely no hearing in this case. It is a matter of debate whether or not Salaita was actually an employee of the university (he had been offered and had signed a contract, but the chancellor voided it). Nonetheless, this stipulation shows the consultative spirit that the chancellor and board of trustees disregarded.

Boards of trustees act to protect overall institutional health; this means they are entrusted with the long-term existence and viability of the university. In this case, the board made a corporate, top-down decision about the educational mission of the university without consulting the faculty. As this decision is entirely undemocratic, it is hard to swallow the board's avowal of commitment to democracy.

It is a troubling reality that university boards of trustees are acting more and more along the lines of the [University of] Illinois board. It is critical to note that many trustees have no background in higher education. They are there primarily to safeguard and grow the endowment—their responsibility is fiduciary, not educational. In these days of diminishing federal research support—especially for public institutions, like the University of Illinois, with strained state budgets—corporate boards with deep pockets and good connections are deemed necessary. But what is startling about the Salaita case is that the board let its protection of the bottom line completely overshadow the university's educational mission.

Money, Not Principle

The board attempted to hide these financial motives behind the notion of "civility" and of protecting students from wayward ideas couched in unappealing language. As I have shown, that is a bogus argument. On Monday *Inside Higher Ed* released information it obtained from a Freedom of Information request, in which we find evidence of emails flying into Chancellor Wise's inbox from students, alumni and parents voicing their displeasure at Salaita's exercises in free speech. At least one sender explicitly identified himself as a donor, touting his "six-figure" contributions. The university president also writes in. Most significantly, perhaps, as *Inside Higher Ed* reports, the fund-raising unit of the university weighs in urgently:

> There is an email from Travis Smith, senior director of development for the University of Illinois Foundation, to Wise, with copies to Molly Tracy, who is in charge of fund-raising for engineering programs, and Dan C. Peterson, vice chancellor for institutional advancement. The email forwards a letter complaining about the Salaita hire. The email from Smith says: "Dan, Molly, and I have just discussed this and believe you need to [redacted]." [The blacked-out portion suggests a phrase is missing, not just a word or two.]

How much did all this pressure influence the chancellor? We can't know for sure, but there is good reason to believe that it made some difference.

Maybe we shouldn't be surprised at this, but that does not mean we should not be outraged. Two things you can easily do are to join 17,000 others and sign the petition demanding Salaita's reinstatement, and donate to his support fund. . . .

What is especially "malicious" in all this (to use the board's language) is the chancellor's and the board's utterly cynical evocations of "human rights" and "democracy" in an act that has stripped Steven Salaita of his rights in the most venal, undemocratic manner possible. Precisely in times of crisis, we need an open and uncensored space for debate. To disingenuously and cynically evoke the "harm principle" in flagrant disregard for the facts, to preemptively base silencing of critics on hypothetical possibilities of harm and to subordinate faculty governance to outside pressure and financial gain show a clear abuse of trust by the university's trustees.

> *"We can grow closer to students when we share a common interest or work on long-term projects, but in every interaction, we remain teacher/student, mentor/mentee, not true friend, and this is wise."*

Students and Teachers Should Not Be Friends

Rick Wormeli

In the following viewpoint, taken from the EdWeek *blog, author and educator Rick Wormeli argues that teachers and students can be friendly with one another and share experiences and interests. However, Wormeli says, teachers always must remain adult authority figures and have a responsibility to consider students' needs and interests first. Wormeli concludes that teachers and students should not develop an equal relationship nor the kind of intimacy necessary for friendship.*

As you read, consider the following questions:

1. What is one topic that Wormeli mentions that teachers should not discuss with students over coffee?

Rick Wormeli, "Response: Can Teachers Be Friends with Students?," *EdWeek* (blog), October 25, 2011. Copyright © 2011 Education Week. Reproduced by permission.

2. What does Wormeli say happens when teachers dress like students?

3. What does Wormeli believe has diminished true friendship?

I used to think teachers could be friends with their students, but then I realized I was confusing, "friend" with "friendly." We can grow closer to students when we share a common interest or work on long-term projects, but in every interaction, we remain teacher/student, mentor/mentee, not true friend, and this is wise.

Adults Have More Authority

As adults, age differences do not matter when designing new instructional programs, hiking mountain trails, or performing together in the same community orchestra. Adult friends have equal power to retain personal identity and shape the course of the friendship, including its dissolution, if necessary. Schoolchildren, however, don't have that equal influence on growing relationships, and they are vulnerable: Adults are in positions of authority, and this asserts greater influence on children than it does on other adults. Unless it's through Big Brother/ Sister programs or something similar, it seems inappropriate for a 25-year-old to spend most of his days in the company of an unrelated 15-year-old in our society.

We look for balance between what to cultivate and what to limit in teacher-student relations. There are boundaries, yet we want to be inviting to students and make sure they know they are good company. For as long as the child is a minor, however, it's not the same as friendships we enjoy with adults. Teachers and students can share an equal interest in local sports teams, for example, trading team updates, retelling great moments in legendary games, and purchasing souvenirs for each other. These are acts of human connection, which is valuable to both parties. Students mature when adults extend

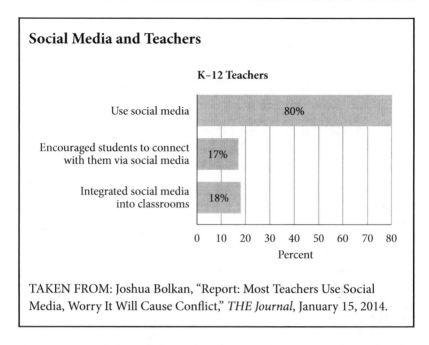

Social Media and Teachers

K–12 Teachers

	Percent
Use social media	80%
Encouraged students to connect with them via social media	17%
Integrated social media into classrooms	18%

0 10 20 30 40 50 60 70 80
Percent

TAKEN FROM: Joshua Bolkan, "Report: Most Teachers Use Social Media, Worry It Will Cause Conflict," *THE Journal*, January 15, 2014.

these connections, and teachers enjoy the camaraderie for the team and seeing students as more than one more paper to grade.

Notice, though, that the teacher does not take the student out for coffee and vent about office politics. There are topics that are inappropriate for teachers to share with students, and such sharing can undermine learning relationships in the classroom, even when the teacher is already very familiar with the student and his family.

Welfare Supersedes Friendship

There are other dynamics at work, too. Clinical social worker Michelle Selby cautions that a teacher disclosing personal information with a student can be helpful when it is to help that student understand something, but never when it is for the purpose of adults filling their own needs, such as when seeking friendship or approval. Her husband, educator Monte Selby, adds, "A health teacher can help kids learn about human sexuality, but it is not appropriate for the same teacher to tell kids which student looks sexy or share intimate details of their own sexuality. Those efforts are attempts to fill adult needs, not support student learning."

While a friend might call us in the middle of the night when something upsets him or her, the teacher who receives such a call from a student remains the concerned mentor, calling the child's parents, health officials, a school counselor, or Child Protective Services after the call, if warranted. Our adult responsibility for the welfare of the child supersedes any element of friendship forged.

Some teachers dress and act like their students in an effort to ingratiate themselves with students. The opposite happens, however. Students prefer teachers to be adults, not overgrown versions of themselves. Students gravitate toward teachers who inspire them to become something more than they are today, not extensions of their current condition. Sure, teachers clown around from time to time, but the better teachers remain clearly adults, facilitating learning, offering insight, and representing larger society as students try on new vocabulary, behaviors, fashions, and politics, watching how we respond.

When we throw a party, we invite friends. When we struggle, friends comfort us. When we are insensitive, friends forgive us. Friends become friends over extended, shared experiences that are not found in 50-minute class periods five times a week. For a student to move from being one of our pupils to being a friend, we need time with one another beyond his school years. We can grow closer when coaching sports teams, directing marching bands, and working on school publications and when sharing segments of our nonschool lives, such as participating in the same church/synagogue/mosque, scout troop, or running club. During these experiences, we genuinely enjoy each other's company, sometimes speak as peers about mutually knowledgeable topics, send cards/emails of healing when one of us is sick, and we cheer from the sidelines when one of us achieves something important. These are humane acts. Are they being friendly? Yes. Are they inappropriate? No. Do they constitute full friendship? No.

Friendly, Not Friends

Teachers and students share small parts of life's journey with one another every day. If they find something in common, are thoughtful toward one another, and through extended time, develop trust beyond that of mere acquaintances, they can't help but become friendly with one another, and this is a good thing. As professionals, we still grade these students without bias, discipline them if they misbehave, and put them in positions of responsibility just as fairly as we ever did before. If they ask intimate questions, we let them know they crossed a line and let them apologize.

I am a better person for having been influenced by the strong character and insight of some of my students over the years. When they became adults, a few of them moved into my circle of good friends. With Facebook turning the word "friend" into a superficial commodity these days, true friendship seems diminished and uncertain. In an increasingly insecure world, we can't afford a policy of "Teachers may never be friendly with students," but we can help teachers and students recognize clear boundaries rightfully established in successful teaching-learning relationships.

We forget sometimes that, while different from an adult friendship, the teacher-student relationship is not a lesser connection. It is often more meaningful and special, with tremendous value to both parties. We try to live up to its promise for the short time we have with our students. A friend taught me this.

> "Without friendship, Olaf's education
> and mine would have been impover-
> ished—and we would both have been
> lonelier, more isolated, less engaged
> with the richness of the worlds around
> us."

Friendships Between Teachers and Students Are Ethical

Amy Shuffelton

*Amy Shuffelton is an assistant professor at the School of Educa-
tion at Loyola University. In the following viewpoint, she argues
that students and teachers can be friends, and in some cases,
should be friends. She says that all friendships involve some inequality of power in some situations and that teachers always
need to balance personal feelings when grading. Not all student-
teacher relationships should be friendships, but when the opportunity arises, such friendships can sometimes benefit teachers,
students, and learning for both. She concludes that this is especially the case given modern childhood, which can be very isolat-
ing, such that children often require adult friends.*

Amy Shuffelton, "On the Ethics of Teacher-Student Friendships," *Philosophy of Education*, 2011. Academia.edu. Copyright © 2011 Philosophy of Education Society. Reproduced by permission.

As you read, consider the following questions:

1. According to the viewpoint, where did Shuffelton meet Olaf?

2. With whom does Shuffelton say student-teacher friendships should start, and why?

3. What examples does Shuffelton give of students who might have trouble finding friends among their peers?

Fifteen years ago, when I was teaching at an elementary school in Krakow, Poland, a student became my friend. I taught his class English in fourth, and then fifth, grade, and he participated in an after-school program I ran. The school was in a gritty industrial suburb of the city, and most of the boys were, in the way of boys of such places, sweet but acquiring a pose of exterior toughness. The boy who became my friend, however, loved butterflies. He also loved art, and after I'd been teaching there for a few months, he stayed after class one day to show me some watercolor paintings he'd made of sunflowers. I loaned him a children's book in English, and in thanks he gave me one of the sunflower paintings that I'd admired. Throughout my year and a half of teaching, he continued to show me his paintings and his photographs of butterflies, and occasionally he'd accompany me to my tram stop, explaining the key geographical features of his neighborhood, like where Tomasz broke his arm and which Dumpster the older boys stood behind to smoke. Once, after some students in his class had been unusually rowdy during their English lesson, he came up to me afterward and told me, "Don't get upset about it. They do that to all the teachers." We never engaged in more conventional friendship activities such as socializing on weekends, sharing a wide range of details of our thoughts and lives, or asking for help with personal problems, but I thought of the relationship as a real friendship and so did Olaf. We stayed in touch over the years, and I last saw Olaf, now 27 and still photographing butterflies, when I was in Krakow last summer.

The Dimensions of Friendship

At the time, the relationship felt ethically unproblematic, but later I began to wonder about the ethical dimensions of teacher-student friendships. Can students and teachers really be *friends* across the barriers posed by unequal authority? What about the teacher's obligation to be impartial? What about the potential negative effects of friendship on student learning? These are serious challenges. Yet, given the amount of time teachers and students spend together, the importance of their relationship to the flourishing of each, and the frequency of failed connections that leave students and teachers feeling misunderstood, disrespected, and unappreciated, teacher-student friendship—a potential balm for such institutional afflictions—begs for consideration. This essay grapples with the most important objections to teacher-student friendship. Ultimately, it argues that although the hazards of such friendships are real, they are not insurmountable. One might then conclude that teacher-student friendships are possible but not worth the risk, but this essay further argues that sometimes the benefits so outweigh those risks that students and teachers not only can, but *should*, be friends. At best, teacher-student friendships may enable teachers and students to flourish in an environment, institutionalized schooling, that too often demoralizes those who spend time there.

Because friendship is a deeply social conception, it will not do to start with too precise a definition. Aristotle's understanding of friendship as reciprocated and mutually recognized wishing the other's good for the other's sake, however, seems to express friendship's core qualities, while still leaving plenty to be shaped by culture. Aristotle famously distinguishes three types of friendship: friendships of utility, pleasure, and virtue. John Cooper calls the third type "character friendship" to better capture the notion that these are intimate, lasting relationships rooted in knowledge and appreciation of the other as a complete human being. Friendship may not be as neatly categorizable as Aristotle suggests, but his types offer two important insights. First, "friendship" covers a wide spectrum of human relationships, including some (for example, fellow citizenship) that modern societies consider impersonal and therefore posing none of the ethical demands of genuine, interpersonal relationships. Second, Aristotle's analysis does mark off certain human relationships, namely character friendships, as especially significant to human flourishing.

Though pleasure and utility friendships are founded on the gains each gets from the other, it bears emphasizing that such friendships do involve a wish for the good of the other that goes beyond self-interest. Because these friendships are based on more tangential, and often fleeting, commonalities and qualities than are character friendships, they are easier to establish than character friendships and involve fewer commitments. If these less demanding relationships are included in the category of "friendship," teachers and students certainly can be friends. Students and teachers often wish the good of the other for the other's sake on the basis of the utility or pleasure they provide, and this is relatively unproblematic. One might even say that it is a problem when students and teachers are *not* friends of this sort. As Cooper emphasizes, such friendships are not simply transactional calculations of favors owed but, rather, involve genuine commitment to the well-being of the other. Many of the ethical problems arising in institutionalized schooling—involving, for example, dishonesty, negligence, apathy, disrespect, and unkindness—take root in teacher-student relationships that are merely instrumental, where genuine mutual concern is lacking.

I suspect most teachers, parents, and students, as well as philosophers, would agree that mutual well-wishing along the lines Aristotle suggests is a far better model for the pedagogical relationship than is the economic calculation suggested by the contemporary logic of assessment-driven school reform. Such a conclusion, however, still leaves hanging the more perplexing question of whether teachers and students can be *character* friends, which is what our word "friendship" generally implies. . . .

Objections

Sex aside, there are at least three good reasons to think that teachers and students cannot be friends. First, the teacher's authority may prevent true friendships with students from ever being established. Second, teachers have an obligation to be impartial, and impartiality conflicts with the demands of friendship. Third, such friendships might interfere with the student's learning.

Are teacher-student friendships even possible? Equality, after all, is usually considered essential for friendship, as it seems to create the grounds for mutual knowledge and genuinely shared experiences. Perhaps the teacher's greater authority, as well as greater age, experience, and knowledge, makes friendship with a student impossible. Perhaps, but not necessarily. As R.S. Downie, Eileen [M.] Loudfoot and Elizabeth Telfer argue, whether or not inequality interferes with the bonds of friendship

> depends on how the parties view the inequality. If one rejoices in it while the other does not . . . then perhaps there is a difference between them which is too major for the sense of a bond to exist. . . . If on the other hand both parties are agreed that there are spheres in which one has the authority, and agreed on the reasons which justify this authority, the inequality, far from preventing the bond, might be an added bond.

Additionally, the differences in authority between persons are so myriad and complex, involving race, social class, gender, educational attainment, life experience—and the list could go on—that if one applies the requirement of equality too stringently, hardly anyone could be friends. In most friendships, I suspect, there is a constant shifting back and forth of authority. In some friendships, one person generally has more but this is viewed as acceptable and justified by both friends. If the teacher did not overreach in her uses of authority (which might entail recognizing the greater authority of the student in some domains), and the student had a basic appreciation of the enterprise of adult authority, they could be friends.

The institutional authority of the teacher does suggest one important limitation on teacher-student friendships, though. Such friendships should start with the student. Before the teacher moves to make the relationship a friendship, she should have good reason to believe that the student is actively seeking a closer relationship. It does sometimes happen that a student will seek out attention from his teacher after class, share details of his life outside of school, and take an interest in the teacher herself, which qualifies as grounds for the teacher to respond with attention, interest, and sharing something more of herself than she does with other students. Of course, the teacher might be misreading the student's intentions, but friendships take time to develop. If the teacher encourages her relationship with this student to develop into a friendship, she must be sensitive along the way to how the relationship affects him.

Grading

A stronger case against teacher-student friendship can be made on the grounds of a teacher's obligation to be impartial. To fulfill the role of a teacher, any teacher must evaluate students impartially, which, besides evaluating students' work, includes assigning praise and blame for classroom situations and assigning roles in classroom activities. When it comes to any kind of evaluation, there does appear to be a conflict between a teacher's inclination—perhaps even obligation, if special commitment to the other's good is part of friendship—to be partial to a student-friend and her duty to be impartial.

Consider, for instance, a teacher grading student papers. Obviously it would be unfair to give her student-friend a higher grade than he deserves, and this would not be good teaching. Besides being unfair to those outside the class who care about grades, such partiality would be unfair to other students in the class, both because suspicion that standards are being applied differently rankles and because other goods (prizes, advancement, college placement, and all the material benefits these bring) correlate with grades. Furthermore, it would be unfair to the student-friend, as well as poor teaching, to give him an unearned grade, since accurate evaluation of one's work is crucial to learning. But say the student has written a bad paper. Won't the teacher be tempted to give it a higher grade than it merits?

There are two ways of understanding this critique. One is that perhaps the teacher is aware that the paper does not deserve a good grade but will give it one. This is indeed a potential problem, but there is no reason to assume that the teacher will do this. Nothing about friendship implies that within the bounds of the relationship all other ethical obligations can be dropped. Nor do character friends necessarily expect that of one another; in such friendships, one of the bases for mutual well-wishing is appreciation of the other's good qualities, for example, honesty and integrity. Additionally, keeping one's feelings out of evaluations is hardly limited to instances of teacher-student friendship, as no matter how impartial teachers strive to be in their affections, inevitably teachers like some students more than others. I suspect all teachers who are honest with themselves can recall instances when they wished they could justify giving particular students higher, or lower, grades. Good teaching always involves overcoming inclinations and preferences, and a good teacher develops this capacity. Finally, grades are not prizes; they are tools for teaching and learning, and ought to be understood as such. If the student and teacher are unable to see grades this way, or do not have a fundamental respect for teaching and learning, then indeed friendship with integrity might be impossible, but many teachers and students do possess ample respect for and understanding of their institutional roles. There are high-stakes situations, such as a make-or-break final exam or a letter of recommendation, when the teacher might have to recuse herself or ask for a second opinion, but if she acts responsibly and the student recognizes that obligation, friendship is possible.

A second version of the critique is that the teacher might not be able to see the student's work for what it is. Maybe friendship will cause the teacher subconsciously to look for its merits and ignore its deficiencies. Or, more insidiously (since the teacher could always ask for a second opinion on a paper), perhaps generally in the classroom the teacher will see only praiseworthy features of the student-friend and be blind to instances when he requires correction. This criticism, however, relies on a questionable assumption: that we cannot see our friends for what they really are. Most philosophical accounts of friendship (starting with Aristotle, but including [Michel de] Montaigne, C.S. Lewis, and other classic texts) present the contrasting view that clarity of vision is one of the essential characteristics of friendship, distinguishing it from romantic love. Reflection on some of our real friendships supports this view, inasmuch as friends are the people to whom we often turn for honest evaluation of our merits and shortcomings. One of the functions of friends is that they give us access to the judgments of the world, tempered by affection, and allow us to adjust our behavior accordingly. The fact that we do turn to friends for evaluation of our behavior, expecting honesty, suggests that friendship and evaluation are not mutually exclusive. . . .

Why Bother?

Teachers, I conclude, can be friends with their students *but it is a demanding relationship, and things can go wrong.* Although the conflict between roles is not insurmountable, problems can arise, perhaps more often than not. So why not recommend that teachers only be caring and friendly, never students' friends?

It might be argued that character friendships are rare and serendipitous enough that every chance to develop one ought to be seized. Some may doubt this, but consider this as well: Children and youth, whose uses of time and space are tightly constricted by adults, have access to a very limited circle of potential friends. Adults who find no friends around them can always pick themselves up and look someplace else—either by moving houses or jobs or by seeking out other company in their spare time. Children cannot. This is especially true of contemporary American children, whose free time is increasingly booked into organized activities composed of age-ranked peers, and who also spend an unprecedented amount of time by themselves. In the past, children were part of wider social life, interacting with adults as well as with fellow children, as they quickly became part of the economic machinery. Since the growth of compulsory schooling, however, children and youth have been confined, for ever increasing amounts of time, in educational institutions that limit children's access to adults, to paid work, to mobility—and thereby to a wider circle of friends. There are some major benefits to structuring children's lives this way, of course, but the drawback—the isolation of childhood—demands consideration.

Most children, of course, find sympathetic peers with whom they can form friendships that are at least sufficient.

Not all do, though. Inasmuch as our friendships are the relationships that reflect us back to ourselves, they are the foundation of identity and play a critical role in human flourishing. The limitations of one's peers are therefore a severe limitation to one's capacities. I am thinking particularly of children who are different from their peers in ways that mark them out for peer disapproval or misunderstanding. LGBT [lesbian, gay, bisexual, and transgender] youth are an important example, as are children who are unusually gifted or talented in contexts where their inquisitiveness and interests are not appreciated. So too are children struggling with a disability or major illness that their peers may be incapable of understanding. I am thinking also of boys in tough neighborhoods who like butterflies, small quirky differences that fall into no sociological or psychological category but merit attention. Friendship with adults opens up possibilities—of growth, of an escape from alienation, of recognition that the world is much bigger than the classroom or neighborhood—that are desperately important to some of these children. There are children who need adult friends—and if friendship with a teacher opens up these possibilities, it would be a mistake to deny it simply because of the risks it poses. The risks of isolation are sometimes far greater.

Sometimes it is enough for adults to crack down on bullying, to address the future, to offer possibilities—but genuine friendship offers a kind of validation that more impersonal supportiveness does not. "Friendship arises out of mere Companionship," says C.S. Lewis,

> when two or more of the companions discover that they have in common some insight or interest or even taste which the others do not share and which, till that moment, each believed to be his own unique treasure (or burden). The typical expression of opening Friendship would be something like "What? You too? I thought I was the only one." . . . It is when two such persons discover one another . . . that

185

Friendship is born. And instantly they stand together in an immense solitude. . . . In this kind of love, as Emerson said, *Do you love me?* means *Do you see the same truth?* . . . Hence, we picture lovers face to face but Friends side by side; their eyes look ahead.

I suspect it is also true, and especially true for children and youth, that maintaining one's clarity of vision without a friend who shares that vision takes an extraordinary persistence, perhaps even a dangerous persistence. Often enough, a truth that no one else can see is merely a dangerous illusion. Without friends, it can be impossible to know which unique insights are valuable, and which are misperceptions to be rejected. Finding others who can see those insights and perhaps offer refinements, adjustments, or new perspectives is both validation of that insight and protection against self-deception. Dialogue is a more reliable path to truth than solitary genius.

Friendship Supports Learning

As this also suggests, true friendship supports learning. Anyone could have praised Olaf's drawings of sunflowers, but his deeper exploration of the arts required a friend. Anyone could have explained to me the Krakow neighborhood landscape, but it took a friend to introduce me to what life felt like for the children who lived there. Without friendship, Olaf's education and mine would have been impoverished—and we would both have been lonelier, more isolated, less engaged with the richness of the worlds around us.

I am not arguing that teachers and students should always be (character) friends, as this would be absurd. But when the opportunity and the need for friendship present themselves, so does a host of possibilities for personal and moral growth for both parties. It would be a mistake to hobble friendship because it might go astray. Human ethical life is full of incommensurable demands and tragic choices. The choice has to be for the better, not for nonexistent perfection, and sometimes teacher-student friendships are the better choice. Facing situations in which friendship may conflict with other ethical commitments, we must respond with judgment, attunement to particulars, and respectful engagement with others—which will sometimes lead us to conclude that friendship between a teacher and student would be unethical, but at other times that friendship between teacher and student is the far better, more ethical response.

| "When I was in college, hooking up with
| professors was more or less part of the
| curriculum."

College Teachers Should Be Allowed to Date Students

Laura Kipnis

*Laura Kipnis is a professor in the Department of Radio/
Television/Film at Northwestern University and the author, most
recently, of* Men: Notes from an Ongoing Investigation. *In the
following viewpoint, she argues that professors and students have
often dated in the past and that they should continue to be allowed to do so. She argues that professors do not have enormous
power over students and that pretending they do infantilizes and
weakens students. She says that new campus restrictions on
professor-student relationships limit freedoms and are an insult
to students, and women, who are assumed to be victims.*

As you read, consider the following questions:

1. According to Kipnis, why did Jane Gallop feel empowered by sleeping with professors?

Laura Kipnis, "Sexual Paranoia Strikes Academe," *Chronicle of Higher Education*, February 27, 2015. Chronicle.com. Copyright © 2015 The Chronicle of Higher Education. Reproduced by permission.

2. What gender asymmetries does Kipnis mention in terms of professors dating students?

3. With what version of feminism does Kipnis say she identifies?

You have to feel a little sorry these days for professors married to their former students. They used to be respectable citizens—leaders in their fields, department chairs, maybe even a dean or two—and now they're abusers of power *avant la lettre* [that is, before the term existed]. I suspect you can barely throw a stone on most campuses around the country without hitting a few of these neo-miscreants. Who knows what coercions they deployed back in the day to corral those students into submission; at least that's the fear evinced by today's new campus dating policies. And think how their kids must feel! A friend of mine is the offspring of such a coupling—does she look at her father a little differently now, I wonder.

The Great Prohibition

It's been barely a year since the Great Prohibition took effect in my own workplace. Before that, students and professors could date whomever we wanted; the next day we were off-limits to one another—*verboten, traife,* dangerous (and perhaps, therefore, all the more alluring).

Of course, the residues of the wild old days are everywhere. On my campus, several such "mixed" couples leap to mind, including female professors wed to former students. Not to mention the legions who've dated a graduate student or two in their day—plenty of female professors in that category, too—in fact, I'm one of them. Don't ask for details. It's one of those things it now behooves one to be reticent about, lest you be branded a predator.

Forgive my slightly mocking tone. I suppose I'm out of step with the new realities because I came of age in a different time, and under a different version of feminism, minus the layers of prohibition and sexual terror surrounding the unequal-power dilemmas of today.

When I was in college, hooking up with professors was more or less part of the curriculum. Admittedly, I went to an art school, and mine was the lucky generation that came of age in that too-brief interregnum after the sexual revolution and before AIDS turned sex into a crime scene replete with perpetrators and victims—back when sex, even when not so great or when people got their feelings hurt, fell under the category of life experience. It's not that I didn't make my share of mistakes, or act stupidly and inchoately, but it was embarrassing, not traumatizing.

As Jane Gallop recalls in *Feminist Accused of Sexual Harassment* (1997), her own generational *cri de coeur* [passionate outcry], sleeping with professors made her feel cocky, not taken advantage of. She admits to seducing more than one of them as a grad student—she wanted to see them naked, she says, as like other men. Lots of smart, ambitious women were doing the same thing, according to her, because it was a way to experience your own power.

But somehow power seemed a lot less powerful back then. The gulf between students and faculty wasn't a shark-filled moat; a misstep wasn't fatal. We partied together, drank and got high together, slept together. The teachers may have been older and more accomplished, but you didn't feel they could take advantage of you because of it. How would they?

The Myth of Power

Which isn't to say that teacher-student relations were guaranteed to turn out well, but then what percentage of romances do? No doubt there were jealousies, sometimes things didn't go the way you wanted—which was probably good training for the rest of life. It was also an excellent education in not taking power too seriously, and I suspect the less seriously you take it, the more strategies you have for contending with it.

It's the fiction of the all-powerful professor embedded in the new campus codes that appalls me. And the kowtowing to the fiction—kowtowing wrapped in a vaguely feminist air of rectitude. If this is feminism, it's feminism hijacked by melodrama. The melodramatic imagination's obsession with helpless victims and powerful predators is what's shaping the conversation of the moment, to the detriment of those whose interests are supposedly being protected, namely students. The result? Students' sense of vulnerability is skyrocketing. . . .

Intergenerational Desire

For myself, I don't much want to date students these days, but it's not like I don't understand the appeal. Recently I was at a book party, and a much younger man, an assistant professor, started a conversation. He reminded me that we'd met a decade or so ago, when he was a grad student—we'd been at some sort of event and sat next to each other. He said he thought we'd been flirting. In fact, he was sure we'd been flirting. I searched my memory. He wasn't in it, though I didn't doubt his recollection; I've been known to flirt. He couldn't believe I didn't remember him. I apologized. He pretended to be miffed. I pretended to be regretful. I asked him about his work. He told me about it, in a charming way. Wait a second, I thought, was he flirting with me now? As an aging biological female, and all too aware of what that means in our culture, I was skeptical. On the heels of doubt came a surge of joy: "Still got it," crowed some perverse inner imp in silent congratulation, jackbooting the reality principle into assent. My psyche broke out the champagne, and all of us were in a far better mood for the rest of the evening.

Intergenerational desire has always been a dilemma as well as an occasion for mutual fascination. Whether or not it's a brilliant move, plenty of professors I know, male and female, have hooked up with students, though informal evidence suggests that female professors do it less, and rarely with undergraduates. (The gender asymmetries here would require a dozen more articles to explicate.) Some of these professors act well, some are jerks, and it would benefit students to learn the identifying marks of the latter breed early on, because postcollegiate life is full of them. I propose a round of mandatory workshops on this useful topic for all students, beginning immediately.

But here's another way to look at it: the *longue durée* [long term]. Societies keep reformulating the kinds of cautionary stories they tell about intergenerational erotics and the catastrophes that result, starting with Oedipus. The details vary; so do the kinds of catastrophes prophesied—once it was plagues and crop failure, these days it's psychological trauma. Even over the past half-century, the story keeps getting reconfigured. In the preceding era, the Freudian [referring to the founder of modern psychology Sigmund Freud] version reigned: Children universally desire their parents, such desires meet up with social prohibitions—the incest taboo—and become repressed. Neurosis ensues.

These days the desire persists, but what's shifted is the direction of the arrows. Now it's parents—or their surrogates, teachers—who do all the desiring; children are conveniently returned to innocence. So long to childhood sexuality, the most irksome part of the Freudian story. So too with the new campus dating codes, which also excise student desire from the story, extending the presumption of the innocent child well into his or her collegiate career. Except that students aren't children.

Among the problems with treating students like children is that they become increasingly childlike in response. The *New York Times Magazine* recently reported on the tangled story of a 21-year-old former Stanford undergraduate suing a 29-year-old tech entrepreneur she'd dated for a year. He'd been a mentor in a business class she was enrolled in, though they'd met long before. They traveled together and spent time with each other's families. Marriage was discussed. After they broke up, she charged that their consensual relationship had actually been psychological kidnapping, and that she'd been raped every time they'd had sex. She seems to regard herself as a helpless child in a woman's body. She demanded that Stanford investigate and is bringing a civil suit against the guy—this despite the fact that her own mother had introduced the couple, approved the relationship every step of the way, and been in more or less constant contact with the suitor.

No doubt some 21-year-olds are fragile and emotionally immature (helicopter parenting probably plays a role), but is this now to be our normative conception of personhood? A 21-year-old incapable of consent? A certain brand of radical feminist—the late Andrea Dworkin, for one—held that women's consent was meaningless in the context of patriarchy, but Dworkin was generally considered an extremist. She'd have been gratified to hear that her convictions had finally gone mainstream, not merely driving campus policy but also shaping the basic social narratives of love and romance in our time.

Abridging Freedom

It used to be said of many enclaves in academe that they were old-boys clubs and testosterone-fueled, no doubt still true of certain disciplines. Thanks to institutional feminism's successes, some tides have turned, meaning that menopausal women now occupy more positions of administrative power, edging out at least some of the old boys and bringing a different hormonal style . . . to bear on policy decisions. And so the pendulum swings, overshooting the middle ground by a hundred miles or so.

The feminism I identified with as a student stressed independence and resilience. In the intervening years, the climate of sanctimony about student vulnerability has grown too thick to penetrate; no one dares question it lest you're labeled anti-feminist. Or worse, a sex criminal. I asked someone on our Faculty Senate if there'd been any pushback when the administration presented the new consensual-relations policy (though by then it was a *fait accompli* [irreversible change]— the senate's role was "advisory").

"I don't quite know how to characterize the willingness of my supposed feminist colleagues to hand over the rights of faculty—women as well as men—to administrators and attorneys in the name of protection from unwanted sexual advances," he said. "I suppose the word would be 'zeal.'" His own view was that the existing sexual-harassment policy already protected students from coercion and a hostile environment; the new rules infantilized students and presumed the guilt of professors. When I asked if I could quote him, he begged for anonymity, fearing vilification from his colleagues.

These are things you're not supposed to say on campuses now. But let's be frank. To begin with, if colleges and universities around the country were in any way serious about policies to prevent sexual assaults, the path is obvious: Don't ban teacher-student romance, ban fraternities. And if we want to limit the potential for sexual favoritism—another rationale often proffered for the new policies—then let's include the institutionalized sexual favoritism of spousal hiring, with trailing spouses getting ranks and perks based on whom they're sleeping with rather than CVs [curricula vitae] alone, and brought in at salaries often dwarfing those of senior and more accomplished colleagues who didn't have the foresight to couple more advantageously.

Lastly: The new codes sweeping American campuses aren't just a striking abridgment of everyone's freedom; they're also intellectually embarrassing. Sexual paranoia reigns; students are trauma cases waiting to happen. If you wanted to produce a pacified, cowering citizenry, this would be the method. And in that sense, we're all the victims.

| "With all the worry about harassment, we need something to stop favoritism."

College Teachers Dating Students Is Unethical

C.T. May

C.T. May is a writer for the Splice Today website. In the following viewpoint, he argues that professors do have power over students and that student harassment complaints may often be justified. As a result, schools need to take steps to protect themselves from lawsuits and need to declare student-teacher relationships out of bounds. May argues that student-professor relationships are also a problem because they raise the question of fairness in grading; students who do not have sex with professors need to be sure that students who do are not being graded more leniently because of the relationship.

As you read, consider the following questions:

1. In what ways could a professor take advantage of a student, in May's view?

2. What does May identify as a divide in feminism?

C.T. May, "When Students and Professors Do It," Splice Today, March 5, 2015. Splicetoday.com. Copyright © 2015 Splice Today. Reproduced by permission.

3. How is our society blind, according to May?

Laura Kipnis is fed up with the panic over professors dating students. She's a professor [at Northwestern University] and knows plenty of marriages that started out with teacher-student macking [flirting]. During the 1970s, she was a college kid and frolicked with her elders: "We partied together, drank and got high together, slept together. The teachers may have been older and more accomplished, but you didn't feel they could take advantage of you because of it. How would they?"

Professors Have Power

I don't say she's wrong, because obviously there are people of her sort. Long legs, erect egos. Give them a chance to get out there and take their bumps; they'll live through it and like the memories. But she's playing dumb with this "How would they?" stuff. It's obvious how the professor could buffalo a student, or have a shot at doing so. Just by knowing more and being somebody who has accomplished a lot, and quite possibly someone who's admired by most people around them. Kipnis quotes her college's new policy and its warnings about "differences in institutional power" and the "inherent risk of coercion." But the rationale is really that a professor is something. A kid may think it's a big deal to sit next to a professor. And maybe it is, maybe the professor genuinely deserves to be seen as a big deal. Meanwhile, his hand is near her knee. Is this a good situation? Yet the rulebook talks about "institutional power" and "inherent risk."

Kipnis figures that underneath this muffled discourse lies melodrama. . . . As Kipnis sees it, belief in this melodrama is taking a toll. "Students' sense of vulnerability is skyrocketing," she says. How did we get here? She gestures toward Title IX [a federal law that prohibits discrimination on basis of sex] and federal punishment of colleges where kids file harassment and assault charges. Feeling her oats, the daredevil feminist gestures toward "institutional feminism" and the fact that "meno-pausal women now occupy more positions of administrative power." In addition, she figures maybe everybody is making everybody else nervous: "These are anxious times for official-dom, and students, too, are increasingly afflicted with the con-dition—after all, anxiety is contagious."

But here are her marquee explanations: "What no one's much saying about the efflorescence of these new policies is the degree to which they expand the power of the institutions themselves." And: "If you wanted to produce a pacified, cower-ing citizenry, this would be the method. And in that sense, we're all the victims." That one is the essay's finish. To connect the dots, I guess what emerges is this: We're all going through a process of mutual cringe. All parties are now quick to call their lawyers, so they scare each other into becoming more rule-bound and protected. The result is that the rules spread through more parts of our lives. Now the college wants to tell people whom to date.

Big picture aside, Kipnis is fed up with people creeping about and acting delicate. "The feminism I identified with as a student stressed independence and resilience," she writes. The divide here has been talked about since the early 90s: Femi-nists who think society, and especially colleges, ought to do something about male rampaging, and feminists who think we ought to proceed on the assumption that girls and women are powerful, self-reliant, springy in the joints and ready to learn. The compromise that has emerged appears to be this: Women do lean on the rules more, but they remind them-selves of their boldness by making greater amounts of noise. For somebody who doesn't like the rules, and is on the wrong side of the noise, this combo is debilitating. Kipnis: "The cli-mate of sanctimony about student vulnerability has grown too thick to penetrate; no one dares question it lest you're labeled antifeminist. Or worse, a sex criminal."

Faculty-Student Relationships Compromise Integrity

Institutions of higher education should also be responsible for creating more adequate policies regarding faculty-student relationships. Only a small minority have banned sexual relationships between teachers and students under their supervision. Common assumptions are that "the urge to merge is powerful," "they're trying to ban love!," and "consensual relationships are none of the university's business." Such views understate the harm of such conduct. Faculty whose self-image and self-interest are at stake may underestimate the pressures that students experience. Regardless of the professor's intentions, students may believe that their acceptance or rejection of sexual overtures will have academic consequences. One study found that close to three-quarters of those who had rejected a faculty member's advances considered them coercive; of those who had sexual relationships with faculty, about half indicated that some degree of coercion was involved. If the professor has any advisory or supervisory authority over the student, both the fact and appearance of academic integrity are in question. The potential for unconscious bias in evaluations, recommendations, and mentoring is inescapable. Even if the faculty member does not in fact offer or deliver special advantages, others may suspect favoritism. The reputation of both parties may be compromised. Faculty-student sexual involvement that poses potential conflicts of interest should be treated accordingly.

Deborah L. Rhode, What Women Want: An Agenda for the Women's Movement. *New York: Oxford University Press, 2014.*

Harassment and Lawsuits

All right. Back to students and teachers. They sometimes bump genitals. Problems result, and the school has to handle the problems. Otherwise someone (most likely the student) will call a lawyer. In the old days, the lawyer went uncalled; not anymore. Kipnis feels that's too bad; when young, she encountered no problems she couldn't handle. Of course, people like that often deserve great respect. But I don't think they're the standard. Other people, often some admirable ones, aren't anywhere that sturdy.

My guess is that Kipnis feels most college harassment charges are bullshit, whereas I suspect they have a good percentage of the genuine, enough to make problems in court. Now the colleges say, "This is why you can't have good things." No more sex for students and professors. Decades of setting up harassment rules, and all they did was dump problems in the colleges' laps. Kipnis sees this as a triumph for antifreedom. It isn't so good, I guess, but it gets the main job done.

Favoritism

And here's the main job: With all the worry about harassment, we need something to stop favoritism. Student-professor affairs have an effect on the students, the great majority of students, who don't sleep with teachers. Because, when it comes to grades, I suspect that the sleepers have a leg up. If they don't, the non-sleepers deserve proof that they don't. Otherwise, the non-sleepers can't assume that anybody is getting a fair grade. Best if no teacher sleeps with any student in his or her department; that's whether or not the teacher is tenured, whether or not the student is an undergrad.

Apparently, all we can do is blunder into this arrangement while trying to avoid harassment cases. So be it. Any society is blind in some interesting ways; here's one of ours. All this talk about sex and none about fairness.

Periodical and Internet Sources Bibliography

The following articles have been selected to supplement the diverse views presented in this chapter.

Mary C. Clement and Katherine Whatley
"Engaging Students: Friendly but Not Their Friend," *Faculty Focus*, May 14, 2013.

Alexandra Rockey Fleming
"Social Media Boundaries: Should Teachers and Students Be 'Friends'?," *Today*, September 18, 2014.

Lori Grisham
"Teachers, Students and Social Media: Where Is the Line?," *USA Today*, April 9, 2014.

Laura Kipnis
"Sexual Paranoia Strikes Academe," *Chronicle of Higher Education*, February 27, 2015.

Richard Laliberte
"Is Social Media Causing Inappropriate Teacher-Student Relationships?," *Family Circle*, November 2013.

Daniel Luzer
"Not So Hot for Teacher," *Pacific Standard*, August 15, 2013.

Doug Oakley, Theresa Harrington, and Sharon Noguchi
"Teachers and Social Media: Trekking on Treacherous Terrain," *San Jose Mercury News*, September 8, 2014.

Mark Schroeder
"Keeping the 'Free' in Teacher Speech Rights: Protecting Teachers and Their Use of Social Media to Communicate with Students Beyond the Schoolhouse Gates," *Richmond Journal of Law & Technology*, February 19, 2013.

S.E. Smith
"Why Teachers Shouldn't Be Friends with Their Students on Facebook," DailyDot, January 9, 2015.

Carol Stabile
"Why Laura Kipnis Is Really, Really Wrong About Teacher-Student Affairs," *Ms.*, March 20, 2015.

For Further Discussion

Chapter 1

1. Jesse Hagopian and John Green argue that teachers' unions promote social justice, while John Hawkins contends that they have done more harm than good for public education. With which viewpoint do you agree more? Why?

2. Susan Troller and Akash Chougule offer differing opinions on whether teachers' unions actually benefit students. Do you think students benefit from the efforts of these unions? Why, or why not?

3. Michael Hiltzik argues that teachers and other public employees should have the right to go on strike. In your opinion, should teachers be able to go on strike? Explain your answer.

Chapter 2

1. Sandra Y.L. Korn argues that teachers involved in the educational organization Teach For America are unprepared to enter classrooms and to educate students. Do you agree with Korn, or do you think Teach For America is beneficial to the American education system? Explain your answer.

2. Eric Charles argues that college adjunct faculty members are treated fairly, while Rebecca Schuman contends that adjuncts are not treated properly and are not given the resources they need to properly educate students. In your opinion, are college adjuncts indeed being treated fairly, or do they deserve better? How does the way adjunct faculty members are treated affect students' education outcomes? Explain.

3. According to Teachers Union Exposed, tenure is making it impossible to fire underperforming teachers so as to improve struggling school districts. Do you agree that tenure has become a problem in American education? Why, or why not?

Chapter 3

1. Do you think teachers should be opposed to standardized testing? Why, or why not? Cite text from the viewpoints in the chapter to support your answer.

2. Robert Prentice argues that teachers cheat on standardized tests because of poor education policy. Do you agree with Prentice's argument? Why, or why not? Offer additional reasons why some teachers might resort to cheating.

3. In your opinion, should teacher pay be directly tied to student test scores? Why, or why not?

Chapter 4

1. Cary Nelson and David Palumbo-Liu take different stances on the question of whether the University of Illinois at Urbana-Champaign was justified in refusing to hire Steven Salaita based on comments he made on social media. Do you think the university made the right decision? Why, or why not? Cite text from the viewpoints to support your answer.

2. Do you think it is ethical for teachers to be friends with their students? Why, or why not? Cite two pros and two cons of student-teacher friendships.

3. In your opinion, is it ethical for college professors to have romantic relationships with students? Explain your answer. Cite two pros and two cons of student-teacher romantic relationships in the college setting.

Organizations to Contact

The editors have compiled the following list of organizations concerned with the issues debated in this book. The descriptions are derived from materials provided by the organizations. All have publications or information available for interested readers. The list was compiled on the date of publication of the present volume; the information provided here may change. Be aware that many organizations take several weeks or longer to respond to inquiries, so allow as much time as possible.

American Federation of Teachers (AFT)
555 New Jersey Avenue NW, Washington, DC   20001
(202) 879-4400
website: www.aft.org

An affiliate of the American Federation of Labor and Congress of Industrial Organizations (AFL-CIO), the American Federation of Teachers (AFT) is a trade union that represents more than one million members nationwide, including workers in education, health care, and public service. AFT's mission is to preserve and strengthen a national commitment to reclaiming the promise of American education. AFT publishes numerous periodicals, including *PSRP Reporter* and *American Educator*. Its website provides press releases, speeches, position papers, teacher guides, webinars, and articles, such as "The Agenda That Saved Public Education," "The Professional Educator," and "The Bargaining Table and Beyond: How the AFT Came to Support Labor-Management Collaboration."

Carnegie Foundation for the Advancement of Teaching
51 Vista Lane, Stanford, CA   94305
(650) 566-5100 • fax: (650) 326-0278
website: www.carnegiefoundation.org

Founded in 1905, the Carnegie Foundation for the Advancement of Teaching is an independent policy and research center that works to improve teaching and learning. The foundation brings together scholars, practitioners, and designers to integrate the discipline of improvement science into education. Its website offers press releases, news articles, videos, and reports. Its *Carnegie Commons* blog features the entries "Learning Our Way into Better Education Systems" and "The Standardization Paradox."

Center for Public Education (CPE)

1680 Duke Street, Alexandria, VA   22314
(703) 838-6722 • fax: (703) 548-5613
e-mail: centerforpubliced@nsba.org
website: www.centerforpubliceducation.org

The Center for Public Education (CPE) is a resource center set up by the National School Boards Association (NSBA). CPE works to provide up-to-date information about public education in an effort to establish more public understanding about America's schools, more community-wide involvement, and better decision making by school leaders on behalf of all students in their classrooms. Among the many articles and reports available at CPE's website are "Defining a 21st Century Education" and "Understanding the Common Core Standards: What They Are—What They Are Not."

Center on Education Policy (CEP)

2129 G Street NW, 1st Floor, Washington, DC   20052
(202) 994-9050 • fax: (202) 994-8859
e-mail: cep-dc@cep-dc.org
website: www.cep-dc.org

The Center on Education Policy (CEP) is a national, independent advocate for public education and for more effective public schools. The organization works on national, state, and local levels to inform the government and the public about the importance of the public education system through its publications, meetings, and presentations. Its website offers articles, reports, news links, and blog posts such as "Empowering Educators to Lead the Way on Data Use" and "Higher Wages Would Attract, Keep Better Teachers."

Higher Education Research Institute (HERI)

3005 Moore Hall, Box 951521, Los Angeles, CA   90095-1521
(310) 825-1925 • fax: (310) 206-2228
e-mail: heri@ucla.edu
website: www.heri.ucla.edu

The Higher Education Research Institute (HERI) is a center for research, evaluation, information, policy studies, and research training in postsecondary education. HERI works in cooperation with institutions of higher education; produces and disseminates original research; provides the resources to utilize research at the institutional level; trains researchers to advance institutional assessment and scholarship; and develops partnerships with higher education organizations to promote institutional excellence. The HERI website provides survey findings, articles, news links, press releases, reports, and infographics concerning teachers and higher education.

International Center for Academic Integrity (ICAI)

126 Hardin Hall, Clemson University
Clemson, SC   29634-5138
(864) 656-1293 • fax: (864) 656-2858
e-mail: CAI-L@clemson.edu
website: www.academicintegrity.org/icai/home.php

The International Center for Academic Integrity (ICAI) was established in 1992 to combat cheating, plagiarism, and academic dishonesty in higher education. It aims to cultivate cultures of integrity in academic communities throughout the world. It provides a forum to promote the values of academic integrity among students, faculty members, teachers, and administrators. Its website offers access to an array of materials that promote integrity at the high school and college level, including "The Fundamental Values of Academic Integrity" and "Honor System for High Schools: A Developmental Flowchart."

National Education Association (NEA)
1201 Sixteenth Street NW, Washington, DC   20036-3290
(202) 833-4000 • fax: (202) 822-7974
website: www.nea.org

Founded in 1857, the National Education Association (NEA) is the nation's largest professional employee organization that is committed to advancing the cause of public education. With three million members, the NEA focuses its energy on improving the quality of teaching, increasing student achievement, and making schools safe places to learn. The NEA's Teacher Leadership Initiative seeks to cultivate teachers as leaders who transform the teaching profession in the best interest of students and enables teachers to play a consequential role in shaping the policies and practices that govern teaching and learning. The *NEA Today* blog offers articles such as "The 'Moral Value' of Teaching: The Missing Link in Teacher Preparation?" and "Top 5 Myths and Lies About Teachers and Their Profession."

National Parent Teacher Association (PTA)
1250 N. Pitt Street, Alexandria, VA   22314
(703)-518-1200 • fax: (703) 836-0942
e-mail: info@pta.org
website: www.pta.org

The National Parent Teacher Association (PTA) is a nonprofit volunteer child advocacy organization that seeks to provide a voice for children everywhere. Composed of parents, educators, students, and other active citizens, the PTA works to improve the education, health, and welfare of American children of every class, color, and creed. As part of its efforts, the PTA publishes informative works, such as *Our Children* magazine, and important, up-to-date stories on its *One Voice* blog.

National School Boards Association (NSBA)
1680 Duke Street, Alexandria, VA   22314
(703) 838-6722 • fax: (703) 683-7590

e-mail: info@nsba.org
website: www.nsba.org

The National School Boards Association (NSBA) is a federation of state school boards that works to ensure that all American children have equal access to quality primary and secondary public school education. It strives to meet this goal through legal counsel, research studies, member programs and services, yearly conferences, and more. In addition, the NSBA provides information on education-related topics such as curriculum development and education legislation through publications such as the *American School Board Journal*. The NSBA website features press releases, reports, videos, and podcasts and provides access to the *NSBAwire*.

US Department of Education

400 Maryland Avenue SW, Washington, DC   20202
(800) 872-5327
website: www.ed.gov

The US Department of Education establishes federal school funding policies, distributes funds, monitors school performance, and enforces federal law on discrimination. It also distributes financial aid to eligible students and oversees research on America's schools to determine the success of educational programs across the country. A range of publications is available on the department's website, including handbooks, research papers, speeches, congressional testimony, and in-depth studies on reform and funding topics. The department also publishes a number of journals and newsletters, including *ED Review* and *Education Research News*.

US House Committee on Education and the Workforce

2176 Rayburn House Office Building, Washington, DC   20515
(202) 225-4527 • fax: (202) 225-9571
website: https://edworkforce.house.gov/

The Committee on Education and the Workforce is a US House of Representatives legislative group tasked with developing policy related to general education and labor matters.

Its aim is to ensure that American students have access to quality education and to provide the tools needed to support work efficiency. As part of its responsibilities, the committee publishes reports, legislation compilations such as the "Higher Education Acts," and other works.

Bibliography of Books

Nina Bascia, ed.   *Teacher Unions in Public Education: Politics, History, and the Future.* New York: Palgrave Macmillan, 2015.

Katherine   *Teach For America and the Struggle*
Crawford-Garrett   *for Urban School Reform: Searching for Agency in an Era of Standardization.* New York: Peter Lang Publishing Inc., 2013.

Linda   *Getting Teacher Evaluation Right:*
Darling-Hammond   *What Really Matters for Effectiveness and Improvement.* New York: Teachers College Press, 2013.

Stephanie Feeney   *Ethics and the Early Childhood*
and Nancy K.   *Educator.* 2nd ed. Washington, DC:
Freeman   National Association for the Education of Young Children, 2012.

Dana Goldstein   *The Teacher Wars: A History of America's Most Embattled Profession.* New York: Doubleday, 2014.

Jesse Hagopian,   *More than a Score: The New Uprising*
ed.   *Against High-Stakes Testing.* Chicago, IL: Haymarket Books, 2014.

Frederick M. Hess   *Common Core Meets Education*
and Michael Q.   *Reform: What It Means for Politics,*
Shane, eds.   *Policy, and the Future of Schooling.* New York: Teachers College Press, 2014.

Anya Kamenetz   *The Test: Why Our Schools Are Obsessed with Standardized Testing—But You Don't Have to Be.* New York: Public Affairs, 2015.

Kevin K. Kumashiro   *Bad Teacher! How Blaming Teachers Distorts the Bigger Picture.* New York: Teachers College Press, 2012.

Heather Kim Lanier   *Teaching in the Terrordome: Two Years in West Baltimore with Teach For America.* Columbia: University of Missouri, 2012.

Joseph P. McDonald   *American School Reform: What Works, What Fails, and Why.* Chicago, IL: University of Chicago Press, 2014.

Michael V. McGill   *Race to the Bottom: Corporate School Reform and the Future of Public Education.* New York: Teachers College Press, 2015.

John Owens   *Confessions of a Bad Teacher: The Shocking Truth from the Front Lines of American Public Education.* Naperville, IL: Sourcebooks Inc., 2013.

Jonna Perrillo   *Uncivil Rights: Teachers, Unions, and Race in the Battle for School Equity.* Chicago, IL: University of Chicago Press, 2012.

Diane Ravitch   *Reign of Error: The Hoax of the Privatization Movement and the Danger to America's Public Schools.* New York: Vintage Books, 2014.

Micah Uetricht — *Strike for America: Chicago Teachers Against Austerity.* New York: Verso, 2014.

Christopher Waller and LaDawn B. Jones — *Cheating but Not Cheated: A Memoir of the Atlanta Public Schools' Cheating Scandal.* Alpharetta, GA: BookLogix, 2015.

William H. Watkins, ed. — *The Assault on Public Education: Confronting the Politics of Corporate School Reform.* New York: Teachers College Press, 2012.

Oscar Weil — *Teachers Beyond the Law: How Teachers Changed Their World.* Bloomington, IN: iUniverse, 2012.

Lois Weiner — *The Future of Our Schools: Teachers Unions and Social Justice.* Chicago, IL: Haymarket Books, 2012.

Jake Whitman — *Destination: Teach For America: Building Leadership, Mastering the Application, Acing the Interviews.* Philadelphia, PA: Pine Street Press, 2012.

Lindsay M. Whorton — *Teachers' Unions and Education Reform in Comparative Contexts.* New York: Routledge. 2015.

Ronald Williamson and J. Howard Johnston — *The School Leader's Guide to Social Media.* New York: Routledge, 2013.

Ernest J. Zarra III   *Teacher-Student Relationships: Crossing into the Emotional, Physical, and Sexual Realms.* Lanham, MD: Rowman & Littlefield Education, 2013.

Index